THE PARADOXICAL EGO

THE PARADOXICAL EGO

Eugene Halliday
and
Zhu Kabere

Melchisedec Press

Melchisedec Press

5 Taylor Road, Altrincham, Cheshire WA14 4LR
melchisedecpress.net
info@melchisedecpress.net

Published in the UK in 2017 by Melchisedec Press

Edited by Zhu Kabere and Hephzibah Yohannan

ISBN 978-1-872240-32-9 (hardback)
ISBN 978-1-872240-33-6 (paperback)
ISBN 978-1-872240-34-3 (ebook)

Printed and bound by Ingram Spark
Set in Baskerville

THE PARADOXICAL EGO

Contents

Introduction

The aim in writing this book is to consider the role of egoic dynamics in the on-going evolution of consciousness.

In a changing world ideas are constantly being re-assessed concerning the phenomena operant both 'outside' or 'within' man. But the interfunction of man and nature means that an absolute separation between such inner and outer aspects is impossible. Therefore we need to review, in a non-dualistic manner, the ideology that concerns the development of the human psyche, the world in which it exists and the interaction between them. The pursuit of this aim is fundamental to the writing of this book.

Throughout this study we observe the way in which every phase in the evolutionary process builds on, and arises out of, those prior to it. In the following chapters we consider how this sequence applies in the development and function of the ego. We examine stages in its development and how in due course, the egoic structure can contribute to an evolution of consciousness that at once affirms and transcends the egoic limits.

On-going evolution applies, not only to the egoic structure, but also to ideas formulated about it. Just as the ego is an evolving functional complex, so are the ideas that relate to and partially constitute it. Hence in this work, although some of the terms used by Freud and other thinkers will be referred to, they will be re-assessed in the light of subsequent relevant discoveries.

A similar process will apply to what is written here. These ideas are being formulated at a certain point in the evolution of man's understanding. Therefore they are offered from that point of view, ready to be revised in due course.

In the meantime, if they provoke discussion and help us look more deeply for the possibilities of understanding the creative power hidden within beings, they will have served their purpose.

Appendum 2017

The text that is the basis of this work was originally completed in 1975 with the working title 'Ego Fulfilled?'

Following the death of Eugene Halliday in 1987 the work lay dormant until the present decade when my continuing contact with the Institute for the Study of Hierological Values (ISHVAL), an educational charity founded by Eugene, prompted me to re-examine and return it to that Society.

In July 2015, twenty-eight years after Eugene's death, ISHVAL closed as a charity, its work being continued by the Eugene Halliday Association (EHA). The EHA has a simplified structure and is as a not-for-profit organisation, run by the former members of ISHVAL. Its objectives are to study and promote the teachings of Eugene Halliday and support individual human development. This edition of 'The Paradoxical Ego' is now shared in co-operation with that aim. It is published by the Melchisedec Press, founded by David Mahlowe to publish the work of Eugene Halliday. The Melchisedec Press is now edited by Hephzibah Yohannan, Eugene Halliday's literary and artistic executor, to whom I have assigned the copyright of this work.

This presentation of 'The Paradoxical Ego', particularly its sentence structure, has been modified in hopes of assisting its accessibility. A new title has also been added. But the insights and ideas shared are those discussed in detail and originally co-written with Eugene.

I am very grateful to Hephzibah Yohannan for her help with the publication of this work.

Zhu Kabere   2017

Chapter 1: What is the Ego?

In order to discuss any subject we need to define the application of terms used in relation to it. We will therefore begin this first chapter by asking what we imply by the term 'ego'.

Long before Freud used this expression it was the Latin word for 'I'. From a very early time the word 'ego' has referred to a zone of individuated experience. But what is 'individuation', and what is its relation to the environment that affords its experience? As we continue this study we will see increasingly that the ego is designed precisely to answer this question. It is a focused zone within a field of power, which by virtue of its definition functions to assess the processes that concern it. Such assessment therefore applies to phenomena both inside and outside relative to its established perimeter.

So let us start by calling the ego a focus for experience. If we are to understand, at least to some degree, the events that go on in life, we require a clear reference from or by which to assess them. This is the ego. It defines a locus, or known zone, that can both push and be pushed in relation to processes going on around it. The ego is therefore a referential structure for assessment of what happens inside or outside its locus. This means that the ego finds out what it is, learns of its own nature, as it functions. Thus the definition of the ego clarifies with its use.

The understanding of what we imply in the term 'ego' therefore develops in every moment of life. We may define an idea of the ego as a focal reference, a zone of self experience. But the sensation, the personal awareness of this zone, will be constantly changing. Let us emphasise early in this study that the ego is not a static form. It is not a structure imprinted in the 'foundation years' and thereby set to run the remainder of its allotted span. Although the ego is defined as a reference of relative stability, the particular sensation of this defined structure varies from moment to moment. And, since observation of such a change also enables assessment of the factors that cause it, the ego is the zone of awareness through and by means of which the environment is assessed.

1

There is an important point to be made here; namely that the ego is a reference for Self experience but is not the totality of the Self. It is a dynamic construct of power, one with particular aims and objectives, likes and dislikes. But the Self is more than the 'unit' to which it refers in this way. The ego is a reference for the Self rather than its definition. But it is through the medium of the ego that we may begin to understand more of the Self that constitutes this egoic reference. The wider understanding of Self that may be found through the egoic vehicle is the aim of this study.

Some people may question the usefulness of such consideration. There are probably many who regard it as 'unhealthy introspection'. But new insight, properly assimilated, can only enhance function. Appropriately used introspection is essential to further development. In short, we can say that either we begin to understand and control egoic processes operant within us, or we are controlled by them. In other words, the possibilities open to us lie between intelligent use and control of the ego, or passivity to its manipulations. The ego is a viable force and it is not somehow switched off or held back if man ignores it. Instead it continues to influence his actions an d he is then passive to its dictates. Thus if greater understanding and control is our aim, we cannot afford to ignore egoic processes.

From modern science we have frequent reminders that the old ideas of a cleavage between matter and non-matter are erroneous. We know now that all matter consists of energy intensified to such a degree that it appears to differentiate solid from non-solid. Similar ideas have been expressed through many centuries prior to their scientific proof. The world's major religions, mythologies, metaphysical poets, and philosophers refer to the origin of the created order in the void, the unseen, or the primal fire, to consider but a few of the concepts put forward. Today the data of science support such insights, reminding us that man, the situation he meets, the forms of the universe and the universe itself, are all manifestations of power within a continuous field of power. We can also say that, not only is the power field able to produce the shapes we know as the forms around us, but it is aware of what it is doing. Hence it is referred to as the sentient power continuum. We shall consider this in more detail as our study continues. Affirming the origin of creation in a power continuum is a primary step in our review of egoic structure and function.

But where, or what, is the ego in relation to this power field? In answer we can simply say that it is the structure designed and posited within such power in order to clarify and express its attributes. That is, it is a functional zone intended to reveal the possibilities of the power continuum in which it exists. Or to put it another way, egoic man is posited for the purposes of evaluation and expression by and within the power that generates all things.

Hence in the word 'I' referring to the sense of self, there is a double application. Its more familiar use is to indicate the particular focus of power with which man identifies, and its apparent capabilities. But at the same time it also refers to the parontic, that is the pre-analytic power, or Supreme Self, which is the awareness of the power continuum and the source of the distinct actions to be derived.

Some people may say that this is confusing and prefer to emphasise the overt physical structures while ignoring their hidden dynamics. But if we seek to understand thoroughly any form or situation we cannot ignore its cause. Insight can never be complete when the factors that cause and control a situation are unheeded. We do not understand a plant merely by assessing its shape, structure and scent. A fuller comprehension depends on seeing it in relation to the seed form from which it grows and the forces that influence its development. Similarly, if we are to discover more of what we imply in using the term 'ego', we need to consider it in relation to the aspects of power that cause it to be.

This does not mean that we are looking for some power that is other than the ego in order to control it. Ontological insight readily refutes such dualistic attitudes often evident, for instance, in some interpretations of religious concepts. Instead we are considering the egoic complex in relation to the control which, because of the fact of the continuum, is inherent within it.

So what is to be our preliminary definition of the ego? That it is a functional zone of power, a means of self understanding, where 'self' refers both to the particular aspect of self posited in time, and the

3

Supreme Self, the Creative Source that is answerable to none other than itself and never inextricably bound by its own creative acts.

At this point we may begin to question the manner in which the ego pursues its investigatory function. First and foremost we can say that it is by self involvement in various situations. A fact fundamental to all experience is that we learn more through direct participation in opposition than by any other means. Whether it is the baby kicking against the amniotic sac itself restrained by the uterine wall, or the adult potholer kicking against the walls of a dark Yorkshire cave, it is the physical opposition that proves the strength, intelligence and sensitivity, or relative lack of these, for the tester. Hence Blake's quote 'Opposition is true friendship'. In any situation we care to examine, we will find that opposition serves a mirroring effect by means of which the self becomes aware of its own causative nature.

This principle is relevant, not only to physical substantial opposition, but also in other realms of experience. Opposition through discussion, comparing one idea with another, reveals both the clarity, or lack of it, and the original intent to define them. Parental opposition, when for example a child decides he need not go to bed, often shows both contesters the strength of the two sides in the dispute. In short, we can say that opposition is fundamental to what we know and that if we were totally devoid of it we would probably know nothing. Whether it is the weight lifter proving his strength, the examinee exposing his knowledge, or the wine taster testing the product of the grapes, setting one sensation against another is fundamental to both the assessment and expression of what is known.

The self awareness of any being is derived in opposition. This is obvious when we push our limbs against an opposing wall; it is less obvious but no less real, when one particular idea is distinguished from many others. But it is even more subtle when we begin to be aware of the initiative power hidden within the idea and the physical form, that is known only by the opposition between its self and the form which causes it to be. But more of this later.

So we now say of the ego that it is the focus of experience posited by Self opposition and that the Self is revealed in the act performed. Thus it is the vehicle for Self understanding. In other words, we discover ourselves in the acts carried out and the ego is at once the expression and proof of the Causal Self. Therefore the term 'ego', meaning 'I', can be applied to the apparent self, the experience acquired and the form constructed, while it also indicates the initiatory or causal aspect of awareness that we may refer to as the Supreme Self. Thus the ego gives evidence of, though it does not constitute, the Causal Self.

It is obviously all too easy to consider the form established and forget the causal power of that form. That is, man can readily identify with the particular experience posited by the Self opposition of the power continuum and forget the initiative aspect of the power that causes the whole process. Consequently, when the 'ego' is mentioned today, it is probably more usual to think of it as the form established and less common to consider, yet alone realize, the cause of that form. The general tendency is to identify with the experience acquired and pay less heed to the motive power that underlies it. Consequently when a man learns a trade such as building he is described as a 'builder', or the woman who focuses her activities on running a home may be known as a 'housewife'. But it is obvious that the attainment of such skills does not mean that they are the limit of the individual's potential. Such examples may sound trivial, but they can indicate a mental attitude which tends to equate a person with proven empirical experience.

Another illustration of this often occurs when social introductions are made with comments such as 'he's an accountant', or 'she's an actress'. It happens frequently, probably because it is a convenient short hand which supplies a relatively easy starter for conversation. In this situation it is obviously useful and social encounters could be difficult without such summaries. But it also illustrates again how easy it is for man to identify with a particular skill. For some people this seems to be relatively acceptable and they appear content to identify others or themselves according to acquired experience. But others, who agree with Socrates that 'the unexamined life is not worth living', prefer to look behind the professional veil towards discovering the motive power that maintains it. They then seek to know not only the outline of their particular image, but also the deeper aspects of themselves that contribute to it.

When we begin to look at the power that acts in and through man, it is apparent that the ideas we hold about ourselves are not optional extras that need play no part in our day to day performance. Ideas, or the relative lack of them, play a major part in determining our behaviour. The way in which political, religious or philosophical codes determine conduct, clearly illustrates this point. People experiencing severe stress have often shown how a personal ideology can assist endurance. Probably most of us have at some time in our lives proved the staying power of an idea and thereby learnt, not only to tolerate, but even to utilise situations that otherwise could have been deeply depressing. This factor has surely played a part in assisting inhabitants of bomb blasted cities devastated in times of war. Obviously ideas, concepts, creeds, call them what we will, have a major effect on human activity. If we express this in more philosophic terms we would say that man's behaviour is moulded by his governing concept. 'As a man thinketh in his heart, so is he'.

If we now apply this to the ideas we hold concerning our 'self', we can say that these ideas have a direct, formative effect on our life experience. In other words, the concepts we hold concerning what we are, will at once influence the activities we perform and the interpretation formed in the process. Hence a belief that we are what we have so far empirically proved we can do, can inhibit wider possibilities of action. We impede our own consciousness if we over identify with prior experience. Whereas in contrast, an attitude orientated to look for greater possibilities of understanding, itself contributes to the goal it seeks.

At this point some people could protest that although they may refer to others or themselves as, for example, a teacher, it is 'only a form of speech' and they 'do not mean' its deeper implications. But if the comment is only produced in response to the challenge, would they otherwise have added it? The so-called 'slips of the tongue' are often unguarded comments that give more evidence of inner processes than relatively reasoned answers. The quick comment associating a person and a proven empirical performance commonly indicates an attitude that is widely prevalent despite the fact that it is both illogical and uneconomic. What any man has so far appeared to prove he can do, does not exhaust the totality of his being possibilities. No matter how

6

great the attainment there is always more to any being than the empirical performance record it has established. To say other than this would deny continuing evolution, which as progress proceeds becomes more, not less, apparent.

There are therefore two main points to be made at the outset of this study of the ego. First, that opposition is fundamental to Self awareness. The second point, which arises out of the first, is that the data so far obtained are a vehicle for progressive understanding rather than its limit. In other words, the ego is the focus of power through which we reflect on ourselves to find out what we are. So we use the ego, like a name, to discover the aspect of ourselves that elects to employ such a referential zone. It is a means of understanding rather than an entirety of the Self, and the opposition of power that generates the ego reveals not only that egoic form, but also the precipitating causal aspect of the power behind it.

Once we begin to consider the nature of being it is readily apparent that we are more than the particular experience embodied in the specific course of an egoic construct. Otherwise, what would cause it to be? First of all there is in us the Will that brings us where we are. Then there are innate feelings, the inborn sensations that underlie the reflex behaviour pattern of each species. Closely allied are preferences acquired by the individual as a result of his personal experience, so that he elects to avoid some situations and repeat others. Next there are thoughts, first of an empirical nature usually related to personal preference. Beyond this there is a movement towards a comprehensive thought structure that begins to integrate personal patterns with those of a wider spectrum. Considering these aspects increasingly draws attention to the cause, or intent, that lies behind all of them. Nothing happens without a cause and no level of awareness can exist without the sanction and support of the inherent causal aspect. All these levels, or modes, of awareness are revealed through the egoic reference of man.

But here again, the experience to which man refers need not be only that of the particular life span with which he is now concerned. Cannot feelings, attitudes and experiences be inherited from our ancestors? Sayings such as 'young Jane has got her Grandmother's temper' are not mere old wives tales with no ontological basis. Today

7

they are part of cytoplasmic inheritance theory. Since physique and psyche are both imprints of power, cannot the genes said to convey physical features also pass on psychological data? If we accept the theories of Jung we would say further that ancestral effects, and the collective unconscious, also influence present attitudes. Ideas of this sort have at times been discounted, by those who prefer not to believe them, on the grounds that they are 'unscientific'. But with the findings of modern science such protests are being steadily discredited. Today we have increasing evidence to remind us that the so-called 'solid, substantial bodies' are condensations of power within a field of power. When we begin to remember that we live within a continuum of power, or as Einstein has called it the 'unifield', it is less difficult to consider the wider influences that are relevant to our present experience. In fact, the possibilities become endless and limiting ourselves to the mere egoic data of a particular life span is a gross denial of our resources.

But at the same time man would be lost if he did not have the egoic reference. It provides a clear focus in what would otherwise be a sea of possibilities.

So the ego, as well as being a potential trap, is of prime importance. It enables man to know who, where and what he is. But in so doing it can easily become the means of confining awareness to very limited horizons.

This is the paradox of the ego. Like a door, it is able to open to wider understanding of its Self and its environment, or it can become an excluding barrier.

After this preliminary review of what we mean when we refer to the ego, we will now move on to consider it in more detail. It can be assessed under five headings, each of which depicts a particular aspect of its activity. These are the formation, furtherance, function, fixation and fulfilment of the ego. Each of these stages will be the subject of the next five chapters.

Chapter 2: The Formation of the Ego

Once again we will start the chapter by clarifying the implications of its title. The word 'formation' is used in two senses which, as we shall see, are absolutely complementary to one another. It is applied to the steps or processes that contribute to the creation of an object or event, and the structure derived as a result. We talk of the formation of a new parliament to describe the voting etc. by which members are elected. But the same term also refers to the house established at its completion. Since development is always an on-going process these two aspects of the term are inseparable. At every stage in its course, the development is generating the form, while the formal result proves the process underlying it. That is, the emergent form at any stage is the evidence of the process that maintains it.

Which means that we cannot separate the aspects of dynamism and defined structure for anything, including the ego. The dual aspects of dynamism and structure are both implied when we refer to the formation of the ego. There is always a co-operation between the dynamism of its formative process and the structure formed by it.

Considerations of the dynamic nature of forms gives a new slant to ideas concerning their apparent stability. A careful look at the ontology of the creative process shows us that a dynamic rather than a static view affords a fuller understanding of what is apparent. Such considerations can greatly challenge an inertic reliance on material 'stability', or indeed on any predominantly formal assessment of structure. Ideas, concepts, are mental forms and an adequate understanding of their meaning requires an insight into the dynamism they denote as well as their formal outline. Any belief or ideology is only vital and fully functional when there is awareness of the dynamics underlying its expression. Or putting this another way, personal stability depends on consciousness of the aspects of power operating now to define an accepted code as well as the structure of beliefs so defined. Of course there is relative stability in any formal definition, but a dynamic process always maintains it and if we forget this we are overruled by inertic adherence to sterile repetition.

9

We are therefore, into the realm of dialectics. Stability, in the ordinary sense in which that word is used, whether it is applied to possessions or principles, in an illusion unless the dynamism that maintains it is also affirmed. Science as well as philosophy supports this fact. Stability depends on dynamism and an ability to assimilate change rather than on adherence to a 'stable' form. Dynamism, not rigidity, is the basis of stability. Any form we care to name is maintained, not merely by the edge that defines it, but by the processes of power that generate it. This dialectical balance of stability in in-stability has concerned philosophers of all ages. And the more we understand it, and its relevance to any formal process, the more stable we become.

So how does this relate to the ego? It means that again we consider the two non-separable aspects implied by the term 'formation' towards a greater insight into, and use of, this structure. The form of the egoic reference that we may define and say 'we know', to at least some degree, is the result in every moment of the dynamism unique to that moment. At no stage in its course is the ego not being formed. As we said in the first chapter, it is not a 'static' form, even if such a possibility could exist. The ego is not like a clock that once wound up may apparently be left to run its course unchecked. The ego is formed and reformed in every moment of its existence.

Therefore let us emphasise as we begin to discuss the formation of the ego that we are not referring merely to a process occurring in early years and thereby establishing a form to operate in later life. The formation here implied is the dynamism operant in every moment of egoic expression. It means that we are taking a dynamic view of the ego. But at the same time we obviously refer to the form posited in the process. A dynamic view does not contradict form, it supports it. So in considering the formation of the ego we will look both at the forces that generate it and the form which results from their operation. That is, we shall assess concurrently the apparent stability of the defined outline, and the dynamism that maintains it.

It is possible so to concentrate on the outline of any form that its inherent forces temporarily lapse from realization. It happens for instance, if we refer to a name, whether of an object we see or our own person, without considering the aspects of power that operate to posit

10

that form. But if we seek a greater degree of self understanding we cannot afford to neglect the awareness of the processes operating now to posit the individuated form of a being and the name we use in relation to it. Fuller understanding requires an awareness of both the name defined and the forces operating to define the named form. It is the growth of such insight, which is our aim as we here consider the 'formation of the ego'.

We have said that the ego is being continually formed and posited within and by the sentient power continuum. From this it follows that the causal dynamism can be assessed in two ways. Whilst there can be an instantaneous awareness of the steps now operant within the power field to posit the egoic zone, there can also be serial stress on the various aspects of the process. Thus the two possible modes of assessment are the immediate comprehensive scan of the Self inholding within the sentient power to generate form, and the focus onto one or another stage in this process. These alternative modes of assessment apply for the evaluation of any form.

If we use the terminology of philosophy at this point we can say that time is a serialised assessment of eternity. The shapes that we see are presented and evaluated in a serial manner in time, yet they are simultaneously an immediate precipitate within the consciousness of the power continuum. Thus the linear stages of a formative process evidence the dynamism that is operant in every moment.

The compaction of power that we may call 'the formation of the ego' is therefore an immediate act of that power. Yet in the course of time its processes are also spread or manifest in a serial manner. Thus when we consider the serial path of the developing ego we may use it as a mirror towards greater insight into the dynamism that is essential and immediate to every moment of its existence. The apparent seriality is due to stress and superstress on aspects of the process, which are essentially co-operant not only in the linear mode, but in every moment.

It is often observed that a similar pattern or process can be seen within the various orders of creation. The correspondence of the solar system and the structure of an atom, or the similarities between the successive phases of world evolution and the development of a human embryo, are examples of this. Whether we take a comprehensive view, scanning the stages co-operant now in a formative process, or stress the serial presentation of one step after another, a similar pattern can be seen.

This is less surprising when we remember that the various aspects of creation originate in the power continuum. Such primal non-dualism is the basis of the correspondence between macrocosmic and microcosmic evolution. It ensures that the steps evident in the slowly progressive evolution of the world and the eras that appear in relation to it, are reiterated in each of the organisms they support. Thus the sequence is reviewed in the creation of each life span, and yet more finely in every moment of such a span. We also see that there is a series of progressive refinement reflecting with increasing speed the steps, or sequence of changes, that are involved in a formative process.

In this chapter we intend to concentrate on the macrocosmic illustrations of this creative cycle. In the next chapter we will focus on its relatively finer manifestations within an individuated being.

But first let us re-emphasize the reciprocal inter-dependence of these aspects. The evolution of the ego cannot be divorced from that of the world. The various creative orders, the star systems, the individuated egoic beings, the singular atoms, are not only distinct images where each depicts in a characteristic manner the involvement of power, they are all in continuous interfunction. No one aspect of creation can be abstracted from its environment. And macrocosmic evolution at once illustrates and directly contributes to the steps of the egoic development.

In all creative processes the two principles that we noted in the first chapter are fundamental: namely that opposition is basic to revelation, and that all such disclosure is progressive. As we continue to consider the formation of the ego and its environment we shall see how these two principles have recurrent application. But let it be stated again that although we may look at the serial presentation of the steps concerned, they are dependent upon and an expression of the immediate application of the will to generate the ego. The serial view is a step towards clarification of the immediate precipitation. If we can remember this while we assess the serial span we are likely to find greater insight into what we have called the dynamism of the immediate egoic formation.

What then can we say of 'evolution', whether of the world in general or the ego in particular? A time biased view is likely to see it as the process whereby forms are progressively adapted to cope more efficiently with their environment. A wider and deeper view sees it as the progressive realization of possibilities which are hidden though actual within the power continuum. Assessed in this way evolution becomes an on-going revelation rather than a struggle for survival.

We can imagine that prior to creation the forms yet to be disclosed are in a state of apparent 'chaos'; that is, they are all present but not distinguished. We may liken it to a picture with a very great number of other pictures superimposed so that the paper becomes black with the confusion of lines and colours. Everything is here but nothing is distinct or clear. In the Genesis account of creation it is described as the 'earth void and without form'. In other religions it is depicted by other symbols. But whatever illustration we use, it comes back to an awareness of a simultaneity of power where every possibility is present but none clarified. Evolution can then be regarded as the progressive emergence of the possibilities hidden though actual within the primary power. This means that the forms created are both new and not-new as they emerge into being and brings us yet again into the realm of dialectics.

From our present point of view we know that in order to know anything there has to be established an edge, a definition, of that which is to be known. Phenomena are only known to exist because of the defining edge around them. Prior to creation they are possibilities of power awaiting further realization, and will only become clear when they stress a defining edge. So the first evidence of the creative process is the intensification of power which, by its self opposition and relative stress in a particular locus, defines its inherent form. The earth's crust and all substantial forms are nothing other than an inholding of power. They exist because of the intent within power to compact to such a degree that the forms generated thereby appear 'solid', that is, resistant to penetration. This immediately discredits the dualistic belief in a fundamental difference between matter and non-matter in the way naïve 'irreducible atom' theory would suggest. The findings of science and logical considerations of the creative process both indicate that matter is not a radically different state from the forces that may impinge on it, but rather that its apparent difference is generated by impaction, or inholding of power that prior to creation appears in a state of confusion and chaos.

And by such self enclosing of power a polarity is established between tight inheld force and that which remains unrestrained. Thus the polarisation affords a contrast whereby the mutually opposed aspects each reveal their relative strength and sensitivity.

But this primary phase of the opposition between the tight enclosure of power and the free, unrestrained aspect, is a state of relative rigidity and progresses very slowly towards the loosening that will, in due time, permit more assessment of the forces involved. The creation of the mineral world, and specifically the earth's crust, is the cardinal symbol of this phase. Its slow evidence of change affords a basis for subsequent stages of development. The 'good grounding' often referred to in colloquial speech as a useful start in many processes, implies such a secure beginning. But in this 'grounding' phase essential to stability, there is comparatively little expression of the data known by opposition. Hence the many poetic references to the silent earth that listens yet keeps her secrets hidden within her. At this stage in the development process the secrets of power remain shrouded in silence.

But the power that generates such mineral rigidity will never be totally inhibited, and in due time, under the influence of what for it must be construed as 'grace', that is the influx of solar radiation, it begins to push through the restraint in the form of vegetation: John Barleycorn resurrected. As with any process, it starts slowly and gains momentum only as it continues. Hence this phase of evolution is very slow. If we look at the estimates of the approximate time spans concerned we may get some idea of the relative intervals. The creation of the earth's crust is estimated to have occurred about 4,000 million years ago, while seaweeds, some of the earliest signs of vegetation, emerge only 600 million years ago. This means that if we consider the time span between the formation of the earth's crust and the present day, 85% of this period passes prior to the appearance of even primitive plant forms. But after this prodigiously prolonged development the next stages are relatively short. Land plants appeared about 400 million years ago, and mammals 200 million. Man arrives much later; his appearance is estimated as merely 2 million years ago.

These figures clearly demonstrate two major features of this process, first the almost unimaginable slowness of its early stages, and second, its gradual acceleration. The seaweeds and plants are the early signs of power breaking through the intense opposition generated in the mineral phase of development. They constitute the primal manifestations of changes that in due course will lead to the formation of egoic man. But the differentiation obviously has a long way to go before that occurs.

After the mineral rigidity, although the emergent forms of plants begin to show more mobility, they continue to act in union with the forces that constitute them. Plants respond completely to the influence of the sun, earth, air and other cosmic forces, and in this sense are entirely passive in their behaviour. In this phase of evolution, the action is corporate and although there is progressive differentiation of formal structures, they are not up-rooting and going their 'own' way. The process shown here is one of compliance between the emergent forms and the intent of the power continuum within and by which they are formed. That is, the harmony of nature is not yet disrupted by individuation. Instead the forms expressed co-operate absolutely with the medium of their development. Such co-operation presents the evidence of the creative intent now beginning to relax the intense, rigid opposition established in the mineral phase. Thus the expression of growth and other forms of movement become more apparent in the plant era.

As in every so called 'phase', the forms that appear are the inner workings of the power continuum. Each stage, or developmental era, is a particular style of activity expressing the differentiating intent of the Absolute. The mineral or plant forms are not therefore merely the structures usually associated with their names, but they are direct expressions of the Absolute intent to manifest in this way. If Western thought inertias assert their hold, it is all too easy to think of minerals and plants as separate entities. But from a wider and deeper point of view we can see that these forms are modalities of power expressed according to the Intentionality of that power. In a precreative phase they are in apparent 'chaos', with components to be distinguished in evolution and a ground of all later ecological problems. It is like the magician producing shapes out of his hat and appearing to create something out of nothing. But in ontological terms that 'no-thing' is the power in which all possibilities exist although not yet manifest. We may liken it to rabbits hidden in the lining of the magician's hat, or in his capacious but invisible pockets. And always, opposition is fundamental to revelation.

The next phase expressed by the evolving power is the emergence through this relative passivity into the more individuated activity shown in the animal forms. At this stage there is more expression of the ability for differentiated structures to get up and go in pursuit of the particular purpose committed to them. Here again, opposition is fundamental to the process. We see this clearly illustrated in the anatomy and physiology of all animal forms. It is the basis of the skeletal system where the pull of muscles against bone enables support and locomotion; in the circulatory system with fluids moving against resisting channels; and in pressure gradients essential to gaseous interchange. Pressure differentials are an essential feature of every living animal, whether it is the osmotic gradient influencing the processes of an amoeba, or the highly differentiated pressures maintained by cardiac pumps. In all systems, pressure, and therefore opposition, is essential to function. In short, this means that if all opposition could somehow vanish, all animal forms would disappear. The structure, function and sensation of any animal are alike dependant on the self opposition of power.

In descriptions of the evolutionary process some animals have been referred to as the 'tool users', a fact alleged to distinguish them from the 'tool makers', or higher evolutes to appear later. Although deeper studies in animal behaviour have shown that this distinction is not entirely valid, it still has a degree of application. It illustrates the capacity in this phase of development for one form to appear to further its own ends by appropriating a substance apparently other than itself and applying it to its own function. A simple example of this is a monkey using a conveniently available stick to reach out for food, or higher evolutes fashioning the tools to help them achieve their goals. These forms of behaviour are obviously further developed with the progress of man.

The way in which animal function is poised between plant and human activity is similarly illustrated by their progressive individuation. We have observed that plants are rooted and particularly compliant with their environment whereas animals show much more ability to mobilise and pursue their own ends. But despite this increased capacity for individual movement, animals generally pursue an established code for their group. That is, they function as the programming of their genus dictates. This can be illustrated dramatically as herds move or birds migrate. We might describe it as evidence of a group mind. It shows the transitional nature of their individuation that at this stage is still group orientated.

Since all these processes are gradual changes within a power continuum, it is sometimes difficult to define a precise point where a particular phase arises. It is like listening for a slowly developing sound; the more sensitive the ear, the sooner the sound is heard. In the present day the ears of man have become muddled and muffled by concepts of materialism, that is, the assumed duality of matter and a force which causes it to be. As long as such a belief holds sway man is less likely to listen for, yet alone hear, the sounds that direct his development.

The ideas held by man, as we have previously noted, play a major part in determining the direction of his orientation. They set a pattern which influences both his perceptions of the environment and the response to what he assumes he sees. An adjustment of ideology can therefore lead to changes both in the sensory inflow and the behavioural outflow. No idea is devoid of sensation since it is itself a formulation of power that is sentient. Ideas are not merely about an awareness to which they point, they are themselves a mode of that awareness. Therefore as an idea begins to dawn in the mind of man the awareness it incorporates is stressed, not as a sensation separate from though indicated by the idea, but as a sensation of the idea. In this way ideas pertaining to evolution within a power continuum themselves convey the awareness they denote. They are not merely signposts towards such awareness, but are more like its couriers.

Thus, in due course, the ideas of a process such as the evolutionary changes now being considered, awaken in man the awareness of which they speak. In this way, through consideration of such ideas, man may become more sensitive and able to feel within his own substance the early signs of the processes that have contributed to his present position. Or in other words, he may learn to hear more clearly the sound that directs his development.

All the phases, mineral, plant, animal, are steps whereby the power continuum moves towards the articulated differentiation to be seen in egoic man. Since every stage has its precursor in the continuum from which it derives, the finer the assessment, the further the roots of the various phases are traced. The animal form is the first to give to empirical ears ready evidence of an ability to hear and move in response to sound, reflecting the heightened differentiation needed for such assessment and apparent response. But in a continuum where everything is in mutual interpenetration, everything hears every sound as its own so that differentiated hearing and reaction is not evident. The progressive distinction of forms within the power field is therefore essential to the manifestation of selective hearing and response. Although such a process is usually first observed in the animal phase, its roots lie earlier and even reach back to the primal continuum. Indeed, some experimenters are now beginning to show that plants hear. So perhaps even the custom of talking to the roses is no longer without scientific backing.

Another feature of the animal phase of activity that we may single out for particular comment is the expression of a sense of possession. Again it of course accompanies the increasing differentiation of defined phenomena. So we see the territory defining and guarding exhibited by many animals. But here again, the preliminary signs of such activity can be seen in earlier stages of development. It could be said that the plants show a similar tendency when, for instance, a privet hedge makes it difficult for other plants to grow in its immediate vicinity. Thus we may see in plants and animals the early signs of behaviour that is to become much more obvious in egoic man. Its precursors are seen here, and very clearly so at times. There can be little doubt concerning the intent of the animal fighting to guard its den and young.

It is interesting to consider the factors that contribute to such possessiveness. We know that the reflex behaviour so clearly shown by animals is based on the protopathic urge to seek pleasure and avoid pain. Perhaps territorial protection is provoked by the same urge. It could be said that the intent to preserve and propagate a species implies pleasure in adhering to a defined locus. That is, preferring to have an edge and avoid a non-defined confusion. This possibility may at first sound trivial, but like the small stream that becomes a raging river, its importance is more evident at a later stage. We will look at this in more detail when we consider the effect such a bias can exert in maintaining egoic identification.

Meanwhile the process of individuation, although far from complete in the animal phase, is increasingly evident particularly in the capacity for selective movement, response to hearing and developing possessiveness. But at the same time the relative lack of differentiation is indicated by the common tendency for animals to function in packs or groups rather than individually. There are, of course, exceptions but that only proves again the transitional nature of each phase. None of these stages are distinct entities; they are processes that manifest the intent of power to differentiate and since all occurs within a power continuum, they pass smoothly from one to another. So between the phases there are shades, and variations of shades, rather than hard and fast distinctions. And in each phase the features can be seen of those that have gone before and those to follow it. The animal phase therefore depicts the combination of rigid support from the mineral processes, and the early signs of movements from the plant era. While the combination of these, together with further differentiation, enables the animal to appear to pursue its own ends. So an animal is enabled to make a more selective response to the environment and, for example, pursue one form of food rather than another. In this way it predicts the evaluation process to be shown supremely in man. But at this stage, since activity remains governed by reflex responses to the surroundings, the differentiated form remains passive to environmental influences.

The next stage is therefore the evolution of the form, which is a modality of power, that is able to make assessment of the environment and move in a manner not necessarily dictated by that environment. Since all forms are evidence of the in-working of the sentient power field, it follows that such a form can only arise when there is a precise, critical balance between the fixation that affords stability and sufficient relaxation to enable exploration of the power continuum. In that situation there is the stability that affords a clear, known reference point, and a loosening that enables assessment of the data available.

This point is reached in the evolution of man.

We are now in a position where we may look in more detail at the factors operant in the transition from clear co-operation with the field power to apparently separatist pursuit. We have seen that the plant era illustrates the obvious compliance between power defined in a formal manner and the forces that impinge on it, while the animal, although it is again controlled by the environment, appears more able to go its 'own' way. It is readily evident that such differentiation is to be further developed in egoic man. But how does this occur?

Since every temporal form originates in the eternal power continuum it follows that there is an eternal, or immediate, correspondent within that power for every form evident in the time process. It we use again the analogy of the magician's hat, we would say that the shapes are hidden within it prior to being pulled out for all to see. The phenomena seen in time are similarly selected and distinguished out of the simultaneity, or co-presentation, of all formal possibilities. This means that the point of view creates the difference.

The time process can be likened to a serial scan, looking at one form after another, rather than at the totality of all forms. The separation of one phase of evolution from another therefore depends on the changing point of view according to which the different manifestations of power are emphasised. Hence there is the possibility of choice between the focus of awareness on one particular form, and awareness of the continuum in which all forms co-operate. And man is the zone of power in which the ability to choose is made evident. He is able to move either in response to his empirically assessed needs, or in compliance with the power field in which he exists. Such choice is made possible by the will to progressive differentiation. As a direct result of this the power continuum can now be viewed from either the holistic or separatist aspect.

This change of emphasis, or differentiated focus, can become a self propagating process. The concentration stresses a particular form, the form in turn facilitates further concentration, and so on. Where the focus is located, to that place will occur a drift of the emotional field. Hence it is very easy for awareness to become increasingly biased, or to look only through the eyes of the form thus defined within the power continuum. It is as if someone wears dark glasses for so long that they forget that they are not always useful, and that new shades could be seen if the tinted lenses were removed. In other words, definition can constitute a trap for egoic awareness, which may come to believe that its delineated, empirically proven point of view is the only one possible to it. In that state it will of course pursue its 'own' ends. But here we are anticipating an aspect of the ego to be discussed more fully in a later chapter of this study.

Considering the evolution of the ego and its environment in this way raises the question, is there a 'gross substantial' change within the power continuum, or is it merely 'apparent'? Are the forms simply hidden or revealed according to where or how we look so that the change is apparent and only substantial in so far as it is apparent? The word 'create' is popularly used to imply that the form so made is a new emergent, or a gross as well as apparent change. But even so, we can say that the form that appears reveals an image pre-existent in the mind of the maker. Or we can take an example from nature noting that the forms that emerge above the earth reveal a pattern sown in the seed. So poppy seeds produce poppies and acorns produce oak trees. In a similar way we can say that the forms appearing in the various phases of evolution, whether mineral, plant, animal or man, reveal the pattern of the form that is pre-existent in the power continuum. In the Christian writings such an idea is expressed in the concept of the Logos, or the precreative word of God, while in Hindu philosophy it is represented as Shabda Brahman, and in ancient Egyptian religion by the god Thoth. These, and similar concepts, depict a simultaneity of sound or form, the contents of which are serialised and so distinguished in time. In this way the eternal contains a forerunner or pre-existent shadow of that which is manifest in the temporal order. This means that the forms when created are both new and not-new; they are not-new in that they represent an eternal actuality; they are new in that they are manifest in a previously unknown form.

Ideas of this sort have at times been associated with a mechanistic view of the universe. Some thinkers have assumed that the presence of a pre-creative template means that there is an established code to which creation must adhere. But this does not follow; although the forms seen depend wholly on the creative intent, the energy of that intent is always free to act as it will. Or to use the words of Lao Tzu, 'the Way conforms to its own nature'.

At this point we have to be careful to avoid dualistic interpretations that would dichotomise the initiative will and compliant form. The will to act is not other than the power in and by which that will is revealed. The dialectic here is that the will, or intent, is free, that is free to act, choose, or initiate, whichever word we like to use for it. While its formal aspect, in compliance with its own will, is committed to absolute obedience. In many religious, mythological or mystical images such interaction of 'will' and 'power' are likened to a Divine marriage, or the Absolute union and inter-function of the two aspects in mutual affirmation. This immediacy of compliance contrasts with the usual idea of the directive and response as serialised with greater or lesser degrees of delay depending on the situation.

Such delay does not have to be. Since the responding power and the initiative power are aspects of the same power continuum, in essence their activity is in absolute co-operation. In that moment the initiative and response are immediate and not separated in the manner usually seen in the course of time. It may be likened to a spouse so sensitive to her partner that she responds as he chooses instead of after the choice is made (noting here that 'spouse' refers to the substantial aspect of power rather than to the so-called 'female' as opposed to 'male' form of mankind).

The apparent separativity of the aspects only appears when we look at them apart and temporarily forget their absolute simultaneity. The principles of logic, the writings of mystics and the references to an awareness of non-duality found in meditation, can be seen as indications of the essential compliance of the power to initiate and the power to respond. But at the same time it is plainly seen that such awareness is widely forgotten in man. There may be glimpses of inspiration, or there may be times when we consider the logical principles that point to the non-duality at the heart of creation, but in the ordinary daily round it is almost entirely forgotten. Consequently man tends to attribute, or even blame his state on society, the climate, politics, or a God-other-than-himself, to name but a few of the common scapegoats.

This is the dualism so prevalent in contemporary Western culture. It goes hand-in-glove with the concept of egoic man as a separate form, determined according to his 'own' particular, acquired empirical data in forgetfulness of his essential co-operation with the power continuum that gives him birth.

In the 'Monadology', Leibniz makes the point that we need to distinguish between 'prolonged unconsciousness' and 'absolute death'. The fact that man has largely forgotten the essential compliance of will and responding power, or of intent and form, does not negate it. At the core of creative power is the absolute, immediate co-operation of the intent of the form and the form of the intent.

But at the same time, we also have to reckon with a decaying after image of previous acts of will. This is the process known as 'inertia', or the persistence of previously established will. It is like the after image formed by the retina of the eye, which briefly retains the picture even though the eyes are closed or redirected. The application of this fact has enabled 'movie' makers to earn huge sums of money. A more philosophic application is to see it as indicative of the way in which a present assessment of a situation is influenced by those that have gone before it. Just as we see through the decaying after image of a prior perception, similarly the phases of the evolutionary process are seen through the experience of previously established data.

The intent of the power continuum that determines creation is free to initiate as it will in the moment of operation, but in full awareness of what is happening now and of what has gone before. It is therefore not mechanistic, but neither is it divorced from the effects of its own activity.

The concepts formed in relation to this interaction depend on the point of view from which they are formulated. Where man is able to reflect on the freely acting will, it is possible to glimpse an immediacy of free action and response. But if he looks instead at the decaying after image, or inertia, of such immediacy, he has a partial, dualistic and mechanistic view of reality. Hence the point of view determines the experience and interpretation of the power continuum.

Thus we come again to the principle emphasised at the beginning of this chapter, that the progressive differentiation of power which constitutes the formation of the ego, may be experienced as an immediate or linear occurrence. The form defined is the result of the dynamics, which, though illustrated serially, are essentially immediate to every moment of formal existence. And the progressive power changes, evident as impaction of minerality, passive movement of vegetation, increasing differentiation of animal forms, and eventually the individuation of egoic man, all depict in a linear manner the processes that are immediately co-operant in the power continuum. In this way the serial order presents an image of the eternal dynamism. And the changes viewed in a linear manner since the genesis of the world illustrate forces that are also operant now, in this moment, in the formation of the egoic reference. Thus the review of macrocosmic evolution can afford insight into the dynamism that serially and immediately constitutes the egoic form. It illustrates the dynamics operant in the course of ego formation, and the forms thereby built into this functional complex.

But we can also consider the process as presented through the relatively smaller unit of the ego thus formulated. Here again, the linear development presents a serial view of stages that are essentially immediate. While the cosmic order gives the grand view, the individual focus represents the process on another scale. First we see a general view of changes through which egoic man is formed within the universe. Once the individuated complex is thus established we may reflect on its further development, presented in this relatively more localised manner, towards a greater understanding of the power that generates it.

This brings us to our next chapter

Chapter 3: The Further Development of the Ego

Having considered the macrocosmic illustrations of processes that contribute to the newly emergent ego, the next step is to look at the factors concerned in its further and relatively more discrete development. As this process, like all others, structures itself on the previously established forms of action, let us first briefly recap the stages already present.

We have looked at the mineral phase as an expression of mass opposition within the power continuum, noting that the use of the term 'mass' or 'mineral' here refers to a particular quality of self opposition of power, and not to a 'solid' somehow fundamentally different from the forces that impinge on it. We are saying that the mineral phase depicts the processes of power operating in such a manner that no movement is visible to the ordinary eye under average conditions. Thus a dynamic stability is established and affords a basis for subsequent expression.

Next we come to the plant era, observing how a relaxation of tenure within the power continuum, and progressive differentiation of its contents, contribute to the appearance of relatively more mobile forms. Hence in plants we see increasing evidence of growth and other modes of formal manipulation. From this stage we move on, with further differentiation and structural mobilisation, to the processes evident as the animal phase.

Thus we gradually approach the possibility of an empirically separatist pursuit. That is the stage where a form is so defined and stressed relative to its environment that it begins to forget its compliance with that medium and assume that it may go its 'own' way.

But such empirical separatist pursuit is not the only functional possibility for the now differentiated form. In later chapters we will look more closely, first at the function performed by the distinct form aware of its interaction with other aspects of the formative power continuum. Secondly, we will assess the factors that influence the decline from such awareness and support the associated pursuit of empirical, separatist prowess. But for either of these possibilities to become substantial the egoic reference has first to be constituted; the furtherance of this process is the concern of the present chapter.

So what may we now say of operations that contribute to the further clarification of the egoic complex? In the previous chapter we referred briefly to the implications of the territorial protection often exhibited by animal forms. Since these are also highly relevant to our present chapter we will now look at them again in more detail.

We have noted recurrently that each stage of evolution arises out of, and structures itself upon, those that precede it. We see this principle reiterated by the way in which processes finding greater stress in earlier phases of development contribute to the ego complex. Let us also remind ourselves yet again that this is not only in the linear sequence, where the earth presents the medium for plants to support first the animals and at a later stage man, but also in the immediate application since all these phases depict processes operant in every moment of egoic function. Thus the activity illustrated in the territorial protection of animals is of direct relevance to the egoic clarification operant now.

The compaction of power that progressively defines the distinct form within the power continuum represents, amongst other possibilities, a concentration of the primary protopathic awareness biased to repeat pleasure and avoid pain. Thus the demarcated form cannot escape the pleasure/pain vectors; they are an inherent aspect of its structure. As we shall see later they can strongly contribute to the over stress on the particular limits that we will call the fixation of the ego. But even if such over stress does not occur they are still present and operative. Thus they contribute to the formation of the ego, whatever its state. Even if man does not identify with the particular experience of his egoic complex, the pleasure/pain vectors continue to play a part in its definition.

The pleasure experienced in operating through a defined locus and thereby proving its apparent capability, is a common occurrence. Probably every man/woman can acknowledge that at some time he/she has known the pleasure that is found in assuming that he/she 'can do' some task. But what does this indicate? And why is it now discussed in relation to the territorial protection shown by animals?

26

If we carefully consider the activity of operating through a defined locus, we can see that it will incur a progressive pleasure/pain bias. The definition of the locus itself emphasises the protopathic awareness of pleasure/pain. Thus when power concentrates to further distinguish a particular form, the inclination to repeat pleasure and avoid pain is correspondingly heightened in the zone being defined. It therefore finds greater pleasure within its limits, and an increased ability to assess, and perhaps avoid, pain. In this way it is possible for it to believe that its pleasure can only increase while the pain could be avoided. Thus, having once found heightened pleasure in operating through the defined locus, there is a greater tendency to repeat this process. And this repetition, at once reinforcing the sense of the defined limits and its heightened capacity for sensory discrimination, again incites its further use. We could call this the 'pleasure in the edge'. It is illustrated by animals fighting to protect territorial gains, by a man preserving his home, or more subtly by a man maintaining his ideology. These are but a few examples of the reflex inclination to guard and re-use established bounds. Such reflex repetition contributes to the continuing development of the egoic reference. It is as if a line is made progressively darker by recurrent tracing so that its course becomes increasingly distinct.

But this is, of course, an ambiguous process since the edge, or perimeter, that heightens pleasure is also the occasion of pain, despite attempts to avert it. The pleasure/pain modalities intensify together. But the manifestation of a negative pain effect is often secondary relative to the acceptable pleasure; a dual effect often illustrated by the 'morning after the night before'. A similar sequence can be seen in many aspects of evolution, when pleasurable vectors receive an initial stress and other factors are assessed later. In accordance with this trend, we will defer further discussion of the effects of intensifying pain until a later chapter of this study.

Continuing an overview of the whole process, we may liken it to scales that are initially balanced due to equal emphasis in both sides, but where shifting goods from one side to the other, no matter how slowly or insidiously, will gradually shift the balance and cause one pan to float firmly down. The formation of the identified zone within the field of consciousness shows similar features. Initially there is an interpenetrating balance, all plans of action are present but distinct components are not yet emphasised by stress. But with the progressive focus onto particular zones of activity, individuation occurs. Thus the forms that appear arise out of those that do not appear. It is not that the now extant forms were not previously present, but that they had not previously acquired sufficient stress to be made apparent. It is the increasing stress, intention, or in-holding of power that generates the distinct forms that we now see around us, whether they are mineral, plant or animal. The intention generates the form, which gradually approaches the point where it can follow its particular pleasure bias and progressively reinforce its integument or other modes of self demarcation.

Thus steadily and surely the defined zone is emphasised and enabled to operate as a distinct unit pursuing its 'own' course. At this point we may call it 'one', since it is operating in an individuated manner. It has now constituted the clarified zone of self-reference, thus affording a new sense of 'I'. Hence the egoic vehicle, the functional complex to which the Self refers, is initiated.

As a direct result of this process a choice is now possible between separatist identification with private pursuit by the clarified zone, or its continuing co-operation with the formative power continuum. In other words, an exclusive identification can now occur, but does not have to be; a choice re-presented in every moment.

The form now distinguished is constantly regenerated within the sentient power continuum. To retain awareness of that continuum would mean a simultaneous consciousness of the form defined and the field of power in and by which it is so defined. If we use again the analogy of the scales, we could say that it is possible to experience the process as a whole, observing and feeling the progressive shift as one scale pan falls and the other rises. Alternatively, we may focus to such a degree on one pan that we define and stress data relevant to that part and reduce the overall understanding of how the transition occurs. In other words, it means we have a choice between seeing reality from either the holistic or separatist point of view. Although such holistic awareness in uncommon in man, this need not deter us from considering its possibility.

The ego is therefore the functional zone clarified within the sentient continuum to such a degree that it may become a vehicle of separatist identification. At this point it will probably help to clarify our concepts if we use the term 'empirical ego' to refer to an exclusive identification with the egoic construct. The use of the word 'empirical' here emphasises that it refers to a reliance on the particular data outlined or accepted as proven by experience. That is, it indicates consciousness so identified with the form now posited that the constituent dynamism is forgotten. It is a shift of awareness to rely on the outline or data defined although, as we noted earlier in our considerations of ego formation, this is but one aspect of creative power. As we continue this study we will therefore use the term 'empirical ego' to denote a reliance on the defined form and relative disregard of the dynamism that maintains it.

So far we have deduced that the ego, and the empirical ego that may arise out of it, are developed by Self opposing of the sentient power field, and that their origin can be traced back through every stage in the evolutionary process. But this is merely the beginning and the ego is now in a position to be further developed, again through opposition, as it interacts with the forces that impinge on its now defined zone.

The evolving power has now reached the point where it has constituted a living organism bounded by an integument, an organism that is an observable phenomenon only because of this integument. The edge formation distinguishes the form and makes it possible to treat it as separate from other organisms now defined as outside its bounds. Hence there is now a closed system capable of interacting with the power from and in which it is demarcated.

From logical principles we can deduce that the input of energy into such a closed system as the now defined empirical egoic zone, cannot produce no effect but will lead to one of two possible results. If the energy constituting the organism is able to assimilate the new input efficiently, there will be little or no change in the exterior. But if it is not able to do this, there will be marked changes within the organism or externally visible, although it might require an expert to detect them.

An example may help to illustrate this point. If a young baby is gently stroked or patted, it shows little or no reaction except that it generally appears more settled than prior to such contact. The energy input here is acceptable to the organism and likely to be indicated by its increasing quiescence. But if the same child becomes too hot the reaction is likely to be very different since in this instance the energy input is more than the body cells can assimilate and a reaction of crying or other signs of distress are likely to develop.

The response depends on the type, intensity and speed of energy input and the capacity of the recipient being to assimilate it. Where such assimilation is not possible the organism reacts with an inner and outer change. It means that if a stimulus is more than a being can accommodate, at that moment the energy will spill out in an overt reaction that contrasts the lack of apparent change when energy input is assimilated on receipt.

It is obvious that if an organism recurrently receives a particular type of stimulus, its behaviour will be modified more by the form and intensity of this input than by other less often received stimuli. This principle has been demonstrated in various learning, advertising or training techniques. A more extreme illustration occurs in brainwashing. Such processes rely for their effect on the fact that repeated stimuli have correspondingly stronger effects on the forces that constitute an organism.

In the generality of man, the stimulus most often received, especially in the early stages of development, is a name. It is by such name repetition that an internal reference is formed within the organism. Recurrently calling a child by its name is an energy input that re-structures forces within the integument in accordance with the name. Those who prefer not to consider ideas of this sort have at times discounted them as 'fanciful', or even 'psychotic'. But the fact that as yet man has not discovered instruments sufficiently sensitive to measure such changes, is not an adequate reason for denying them. If we remember that the soma of man is not a solid somehow fundamentally different from his psyche, the structuring effect of sound is less difficult to consider. Scientific endorsement is also evident in the Chladni figures.

30

We can therefore say, with personal, scientific and logical support, that naming a child is not merely a social convenience, but it is a contributory factor in the child's development. Each repetition of the name adds to the inner reference being established within the organism. We could liken it to a main stream developing within the psyche and increasingly channelling the forces operant within the being. When other stimuli are received they will then either assimilate to this structure and so support the egoic mass, or they will fail to do so and set up alien centres within the organism. The naming process is therefore of fundamental importance in establishing egoic awareness and progressively builds up a stable reference within the emergent form.

The positive progress of this process is contrasted by the outcome when this cycle is not firmly established. If the appropriate attention and name reiteration is severely lacking or not received, the ego complex will not be suitably reinforced and individual awareness can be hampered. A gross deficiency of the process can afford a psychodynamic reason for the 'ego disintegration' said by some psychiatrists to occur in patients with schizophrenia when the awareness of a personal name and location are temporarily lost.

So what are the forces that feed the 'egoic mass'? First and foremost, they include repetition of the name adopted by the child. But in addition to this, the child will integrate to this name structure the data acquired while, operating through the vehicle now accepting the name, he/she explores the environment. In the early stages of development children frequently repeat their name instead of using personal pronouns so that we hear phrases like 'Tommy wants it', or 'that's Tommy's car'. It is at a later stage that we hear 'I want it', or 'that's mine'. But whether the name is explicit or implicit, the associated data are held and may be expressed in association with that name. Thus the forces integrated into the egoic mass are not only the name repetition, but the data acquired from experience while using that name, whether or not it is overtly expressed.

The data derived from any mode of action can be assimilated to the ego provided they are received at an appropriate rate. The experience may concern mechanical ability, for instance using constructional toys; sensory assessment such as learning that fires are warm or even hot; or concept formation, for example learning names for objects encountered. Provided such data are received at an assimilable rate, they can integrate to the egoic mass. Hence, in addition to the name form, the consciousness now resonating with that name progressively accepts more data pertaining to its environment.

This process includes rational formulation, and feeling evaluation of the acts performed. That is, assimilation of data to the egoic mass requires the co-operation of the three aspects of consciousness referred to as action, formulation and sensation. The degree of assimilation will vary according to the extent to which these aspects are harmonised in a particular event. High degrees of assimilation occur when many of the facets of an act are appropriately felt and adequately defined. But with lesser degrees of such co-ordination, much or even most of the energy operant at that moment by-passes rational analysis and becomes a sub-cortical, or sub-egoic, imprint within the organism. We will consider the subsequent effects of such sub-rational programming in more detail later in this chapter. It is only mentioned briefly at this point to highlight its contrast with the rational processes operant in, and further defining, the egoic structure.

The other organisms most influential in the formation of the ego mass, that is the impaction of power aligned to the name, are usually the parents and parent substitutes. After them, it is likely that close associates such as family, friends, educators, and other regular group members, assert the main influence. Their repetition of the child's name together with other assimilable data, such as, 'John's a good boy', 'Jill's a happy girl', especially when they are supported by the approval of the Mother, will continue to reinforce the egoic mass.

But in contrast to such progressive support there can be contrary opposing pressures. For instance, contrary imprints can occur when a child encounters signs of disapproval or painful stimuli that he/she will not naturally assimilate to the emerging ego. A more specific example would be the effect incurred if a child is severely punished and the energy input is too strong, too intense, or of an alien character and therefore cannot be assimilated by the organism at that stage. This unassimilated energy may be partly dissipated in overt behaviour, but it can also set up invert responses, some of which may develop contrary centres within the organism not in accordance with the main egoic imprint. Thus areas of resistance can be established that will subsequently challenge the egoic intent. We may liken such disparate imprints to deserters from an established army who may join an alien force. But overall, the ego usually remains the dominant influence and becomes increasingly strongly established as the chief reference centre within the organism so that the life forces of the child operate more through this than through any other channel.

This means that egoic development is a self propagating process. Once established, the energy operating through this channel assimilates further data to it and so increases its dominance. This effect is comparable to that of a large river pulling other streams into its flow and increasing its thrust. In this way the main stream of the egoic 'self image' is progressively established. It is a process that is fundamental to an individual's awareness of 'self' within the power continuum that constitutes all things.

Considering egoic development in this way has at times led to questions about painful naming rites, since it might appear that the infliction of pain could undermine the emergent ego. But if we examine this more closely we will see, not only that this does not happen, but also that the various aspects of this process can be mutually supporting.

When a child is given a name, especially with clear parental endorsement, the spoken name is usually acceptable to the egoic mass. But if at the same time a pain producing act, such as circumcision, is performed, while the name is assimilated to the ego, the unassimilable pain sets up a sub-cortical, or sub-rational, imprint that is also resonating with the name. Thus, in this instance, sub-rational data are established which, though not assimilated to the egoic structure, are also resonating with the name accepted by that ego form. This means that established within the child there is now a conscious acceptance of the name assimilated to the egoic mass, and co-operant with it, a sub-rational imprint reinforcing it through fear. In this way a pain-provoking rite can support rather than undermine the structure of the ego.

After this initial analysis of the role played by these factors in the development of the ego, we will now take a closer look at the effects of energy input into the organism now constituted and what we mean when we talk of the integration of data to the egoic mass.

The Freudian model describes the ego as the result of 'reality testing', or putting it another way, as the growing understanding attained by an individual as he/she explores 'reality' finding out what he/she can, or cannot do. The limit testing by children, seeing just how far they can go before they are checked, whether by parental restraint or physical restriction, is an example of this sort of thing. The data derived from such environmental exploration, provided they come at an assimilable rate, further structure the egoic awareness. We might describe it as the egoic 'data bank'.

But it is not only physical restraint, or spoken prohibition, with which the being comes into conflict. Freud also made recurrent reference to the effect of ideology, or the 'superego', in the continuing development of man. He described a triad of factors that influence the personality throughout its early and subsequent stages of formation. He described this triad as the 'id, the ego and the superego'. He used the term 'id' to refer to the impulsive drive of the organism. Pursuit of this drive, and meeting the 'reality principle', then led to the formation of the 'ego', that is the resulting data and structuring of consciousness relating to what activity can or cannot be performed. He deduced that the third stage, the superego, was then constituted when, in addition to what is possible, the individual clarified his personal goals and ideals in terms of what is permissible. Freud observed two modalities within this aspect of human consciousness. One being, the 'ego-ideal', that is the standard which the being for some particular reason would like to attain. The other aspect being the 'conscience', the conduct which, again for personal reasons, the being decides it ought to restrain. It is readily apparent that such standards are determined by the personal inclination of each individual, otherwise every man would have similar aspirations and taboos, which clearly does not happen.

Thus the superego becomes a particular construct arising out of the egoic data formed as the individual pursues its inherent drive to act in particular ways. But this means that the superego is now in a position to feed back and influence egoic activity. Particular effects it can exert include prohibiting concrete investigation of experience deemed 'unsuitable', and prejudicing the interpretation of data that have been allowed. An example of the first of these possibilities is sexual limitation and perhaps denial. The second possibility is shown in the differing assessments that can be formed of speeding on a motorway. To one person it can be exhilarating but to another a cause of considerable fear. If we look carefully at man's assessments of his personal behaviour, we can observe that it is likely to be strongly influenced by previously established ideals. Although a person may claim to make an 'unbiased' appraisal of a situation, it is much more likely that he has not admitted to the preferences and prohibitions hidden yet operant in his actions.

The ego unit, while investigating the reality principle, can therefore be deemed to stand between the impulsive urge of the id on one side, and the restraint or direction of the superego on the other side. Hence, it has been likened to a referee within a person when the id drives, the superego dictates and the ego decides. In psychology lectures in the 1970's this triad was likened to the interaction between a terrified bank-clerk (the ego), shut in a cellar (man) and required to referee a fight between a prim and proper spinster (the superego) and a sex-starved chimpanzee (the id). It aptly illustrated the point.

But we need not confine ourselves to Freudian phraseology when we consider the dynamic interaction of these aspects of being. The terminology of Indian philosophy is also helpful in this process. Here the term 'pra-' refers to the rational restraint, and 'na-' to the impulsive life force. With the two together we have 'prana', that is, the vital breath of man. Or, in other words, man knows he is a living being because of the interaction of these opposing aspects within him.

The models of Freud, Indian philosophy, and many other expressions of insight, illustrate the ego as a zone of conflict stretched between the opposing impulse and rational restraint, or pra-na. They imply that an energy input received by the egoic construct is to be balanced between the responsive urge, or what the being would automatically do about it, the dictates of reason or what it believes it 'ought' to do about it, and what the practical extant situation permits. If the energy input is at a rate that permits assessment and a balanced response, at that moment it is acted on and integrated into the egoic structure.

But the situation is very different if the energy input is not assimilable when it is acquired. In that event, neither the stimulus received, or the reactions provoked are adequately analysed and the activity lacks co-ordination. The forces of being are therefore less controlled and a disturbance of mood, mentation or mechanical ability may be seen. That is, if the energy input is more than the being can accommodate at that moment, instead of appropriate analysis and a balanced response, there occurs a relatively uncontrolled physical or emotive expression.

In such a state of comparative disarray the sub-cortical imprints, to which we have referred briefly earlier in this chapter, are likely to acquire greater stress. This is particularly so if there is an affinity between the uncontrolled input of energy and a prior conditioning of the being. It is obvious that some encounters are more disruptive than others and that no two beings react equally to the same stimulus. A person who has been primed by a previous experience, such as severe pain, is particularly likely to react noticeably on meeting a situation similar to that which originally proved painful to him.

Such retention of emotive imprints relating to prior experience is easier to understand when we remember that the body of man is a condensation of power and not a gross material fundamentally different from his psyche. The changes of the psychic structures can directly influence the physical aspect of being. It is very easy for man to establish a record of an emotive response that lacks adequate rational analysis. Such imprinted data then constitute a non-integrated sensory memory, so that the being knows, for instance, the pain reaction, but is not clearly aware of its precise cause and is likely to retreat from situations with similarities to the prior precipitant even though they are not equivalent.

This process commonly affords a basis for various modes of conditioning operant in man. The imprinted data thus retained in an inadequately co-ordinated manner readily become a foundation for non-rational responses later in life. Let us use an example to illustrate what is implied here. A child who is severely frightened by a dog is unlikely to integrate fully the energy response to the situation. Instead he could easily retain an unclarified, but fear laden imprint vaguely associated with dogs. If he later meets a situation such as another dog being exercised under the control of its owner, although in itself this is not a threatening scenario, if it has sufficient similarity to the child's prior encounter it can re-evoke the sensation of fear. This type of response illustrates how an emotive response to a previous event can be projected onto a present happening even though it does not necessarily belong there. This happens because in both the original and present encounters the organism does not have enough control to assess and correctly integrate the reactive energy. Data such as these are not, strictly speaking, egoic; they are sub-egoic. But, if they are subsequently re-assessed by the individual so that he consciously defines where the reactions arose and integrates the sensation involved with clear defining reasons, they then become part of the egoic data bank. Such re-assessment and re-alignment releases an individual from data that could otherwise incur emotional bias and personal prejudice.

So far we have tended to emphasise the personal dynamics of the ego. But group interactions and dynamics are also relevant here. In the continuing development of the ego mass many of the stimuli received come from other beings within a particular group and act on the recipient protoplasmic mass to induce it to modify its behaviour in accordance with the ethics of that group. An obvious example of this is the moral conditioning that parents and elders may apply to children. It gradually constitutes the so-called 'ethical' or 'moral' consciousness. That is, the training of the ego to co-ordinate with a contemporary group behaviour pattern.

The development of the ego is therefore influenced by both individual and group conduct. Which means that again we can see evidence here of the ego recapping experience that has received greater stress in earlier phases of evolution. We noted that in the animal phase there is a movement towards individuation, while in man that critical balance is reached that enables an expression of individual as well as corporate action. The tendency, for instance in tribal conduct, to act as a group rather than as individuals pursuing separate courses, can be seen as a re-statement of the less individuated phases of development. It reminds us again that each stage of evolution is founded on the experience of those before it, or to put it in more poetic terms, every universe is founded on the debris of a prior universe.

The German word 'aufgehoben' expresses this idea exactly. It means that each phase arises out of, constructs itself upon, and lifts up, those that precede it. Unfortunately there is not an English word that adequately interprets this. In translation of Kierkegaard's writings 'annulled' is sometimes used for it. But this is not its full meaning, since the subsequent development recaps and uses, as well as annuls, the processes of the prior phases.

In this chapter we have considered how it is possible to trace the changes concerned in the initial formation of the ego and its further development right back through the evolutionary cycle. Every stage or form of power presented in and through the universe arises out of processes that precede it, and egoic man is no exception to this principle. If we also remember that the serial is an image of the dynamism that is immediate to any creative expression, we can say further that the ego is being formed in every moment of its existence by the power operating in the manner illustrated by the multilinear progression.

The ego is not, therefore, merely a product of any one particular process predominant at a certain stage in its development, but it is continually maintained by the interfunction of all its contributory processes. Events long past and recent are all relevant. The ego is the individuated functional complex towards which every step in the creative cycle can be seen as progressing, both serially and immediately. Although each phase of development can be considered as relatively distinct, there is always co-operation as the various stages conspire to generate the individuated complex. The linear series illustrates the immediate dynamism of the power continuum by means of which a distinct zone of operation is progressively focused and brought to the position where it can be used to evaluate and express data that pertain to it.

This brings us to our next chapter where we consider the function of the ego.

Chapter 4: The Function of the Ego

In any structure that we carefully examine, we will see the close liaison that exists between form and function. The ego is no exception. In fact we can call them dual aspects of a unity, since the form is the form of the function and the function is the function of the form. They are not separate in any way. We only consider them as if they are separate in order to clarify their features. So in studying the initial formation and further development of the ego, we are also clarifying its function.

As we noted earlier, form is not a static creation somehow energised by a power that enters into it. Form and function are both dynamic; the form is the outline or shape of the process, while the function is the expression of the dynamism that operates through it modifying both the form concerned and the medium in which that form exists. There is no such thing as a non-functional form. Since all things that exist are maintained by and within the power continuum, any form has a direct effect on all other processes and this is its function.

When the heart pumps the blood around the vascular system, or the bones oppose the pull of muscles, it is not only the structures directly involved that experience the effects, but indirectly the whole body. These examples are obvious, but if we deduce the logical implications of the fact of the power continuum, we have to say that similarly every form feels, to some degree, the experience of other activities within this power field.

In meditation exercises it is at times possible to begin to sense comprehensively such interpenetration of all things. In Zen Buddhism it is described as 'Jijimuge'. Whether we approach such awareness through logical analysis, sensory change, or both of these, the fact remains that the reciprocal interpenetration of all forms and their functional possibilities is the essence of creation. But having said this, it follows that within such continuity of awareness a clear understanding depends on a clear focal zone though which to experience it. Thus we come to the function of the ego.

To refer to the continuum in this way does not imply an escape into a non-individuated nebulous bliss. It is a means of seeking to understand the interrelation of the particular zone within the wholeness of power that constitutes it. Thus it is aiming at a more conscious use of the distinguishing element, or its true operation, rather than its denial. We can say that the empirical ego functions as a zone of reference aiding both the analysis and synthesis of the aspects of consciousness operant within and through it. And since it is continually maintained by the interaction of all levels of consciousness, that the full realization of its function cannot imply less than immediate awareness of their origin and application within the power continuum.

Thus at the beginning of our review of egoic function we have a preliminary definition of the process. We can say that the egoic unit is designed so to investigate reality that it continually rediscovers its origin and the creative intent that causes it to be. But intention is only fully revealed when an act is completed. So we can say further that there is a reciprocal interrelation between a thorough clarification of form and rediscovery of the creative intent. The ego is therefore designed to assess and express the data of the universe with such precision as will afford a heightened awareness of the forms defined and their defining intent.

Therefore we come again to the principle that we are concerned with dynamic intentionality rather than merely formal analysis. That the ego experiences and assesses formal constructs is readily evident. But here we are also seeking to reflect on such formulation towards discerning the functional intent that controls it.

Form is power behaving in a self-structuring manner; the primary analysis performed through the egoic formulation progressively supports this awareness. The aspects of the process are being clarified in and through the egoic complex by a direct experience of the operation. Or in other words, we learn of the creative intent through personal commitment and reflexion.

We have said that the creation of all forms is due to impaction of the power of the continuum. This means that there is no form that is absolutely divorced from its awareness, or, in other words, that the awareness of the continuum is the essence of every form or event that is defined. This insight implies that at the heart of every form is a consciousness not separate from any aspect of reality and that this is the basis of immediate recognition of the dynamism operant in forms apparently peripheral to an observant being.

But there is also another basis for the understanding of such reciprocity. In the previous chapters we referred recurrently to the similarities between steps in the creative cycles of the macrocosm and the microcosm. In both of these a basic plan can be seen in the progressive impaction of power presented as a linear series. Although there are of course differences, at the same time the stages evident in the intensification of power as the possible becomes substantial are reiterated in every form that is manifest whether this occurs on the grand macrocosmic scale or within smaller microcosms. Hence, one form can recognise the experience of another because in its own development it knows a similar occurrence. Thus the reciprocity of awareness between processes defined as inner or outer relative to the empirical ego, can be attributed either to the immediate non-dual awareness of the continuum, or the serial experience of similar and related processes.

We are now moving into the realms of epistemology, or the basis on which we say we 'know' what we 'know'. Such assessments are founded on convergence between processes occurring outside the integument of the assessor with those internal to his person. When we touch a hot surface our fingers feel the heat, on lifting a heavy basket our shoulders usually feel the strain. Similarly, if we encounter a new idea an inner process is likely to interpret it as 'true' or 'false' in relation to already existent internal structures. In any assessment we make there is an inner change which enables us to assert that we 'know' what we so claim.

Thus the resonance between inner and outer aspects of our experience, or a two-way observation, is the basis of our apparent knowledge. That is, a being knows only the modifications of its own substance. And it is through encounters with other forms around him that egoic man learns, not only the characteristics of apparently alien forms, but of formalising processes within his own being. It is obvious that by observation from his defined point of view egoic man is able to

41

assess objects and situations he meets. But what we are saying here is that at the same time he can, if he so chooses, use these to reflect on his own inner dynamism, that is, the processes that now enable him to make whatever assessments are made. And through all of this activity, again if he so chooses, as he pursues his functional possibilities, he can seek awareness of the intent that underlies all such function.

We can therefore say that the ego is designed to break the tyranny of form. That is, it is to see through an over reliance on formal definition and become increasingly aware of the causal consciousness that maintains it. This brings us again to the paradox of the ego, since the formal vehicle of the ego is used in this form breaking process. But it means, as we have previously noted, looking into and through the form rather than merely at its boundaries.

In the data derived by means of the egoic zone, we are seeking, through the formulations that are made, an understanding of other aspects of power operant within them. This point is not often expressed in contemporary society with its usual stress on the 'form of law', 'form of knowledge', 'formal examinations' and even 'form of art'. In fact, it can be said that we are now experiencing an era of which its civilisation is an ever-increasing formulation. Of course we require forms for reference, this is so obvious that it hardly needs stating. But they are only for reference and not an end to which consciousness intends to bind itself. And the egoic data bank, to which we referred in the previous chapter, has to be approached in this way. The assessments for which the egoic unit is designed concern all the modalities of power revealed in and through the data now discernible.

Having considered rather briefly the possibilities of recognition by immediate or serial assessments, let us now look at this in more detail. We have seen that the ego, like all other encapsulated forms, is defined by the progressive concentration of power within the sentient continuum. This fact has two major implications that may be noted at this point; first, that although there is formal and functional differentiation, every form defined has within it an essence of awareness not absolutely alien to other forms; and secondly, that all forms are sentient. The apparent divisions are due to relative stress, or superstress, rather than absolute dichotomy and each form can be aware of the activity of other forms. This reiterates a point made in an earlier chapter, that the differences established are due to discriminative focus within the power field.

It follows from this observation that the events which the egoic zone is designed to evaluate can be known for two reasons. Firstly because the ego itself goes through a similar process, that is, traverses stages of a like manner to arrive at its present state of being. Secondly, because of the immediate resonance operant in sentient power which, when it is let loose, enables a 'now' awareness of continuity.

Therefore it is possible for the ego to feel and thus to know what happens around it both by virtue of sharing a similar developmental process, and by an immediate interaction in this moment of time. These aspects co-operate in enabling the egoic zone to assess data, that is the processes of power, within the universe.

The ego is not some sort of onlooker; it knows by participation. The ego, as we noted at the beginning of this chapter, assesses events around it by their resonance with its own inner dynamism. The evaluation performed through the ego is based on a correspondence between events around and those internal to the perceiving being. Hence, as we said earlier, a being knows what it knows through the modifications of its own substance.

The evaluatory function of the ego is therefore based on a type of mirror imaging rather than the calculations of a detached observer. Obviously an experience of this type will afford a depth of understanding greater than would be obtained by a distant appraisal. We often talk of the value of 'first hand experience', or use expressions like 'I know what it is like, I have been through a similar situation myself'. Colloquial sayings such as these illustrate the greater reliance placed on direct, personal participation in an activity.

A similar principle applies to egoic function. It is enabled to make a more thorough assessment of the data available to it simply because it shares, rather than merely sees, the events concerned. But let it be emphasised that this is not only the relatively superficial type of sharing often implied when, for instance, two men with mumps both assume they know the experience of the other one. It is more than this.

The sharing we are referring to here is the essential interpenetration of all forms within the power continuum. That is, it is based on immediate co-function as well as serial similarity. It affirms that even when linear steps appear to be similar for two individuals, the similarity of perception is not merely due to like steps on a path of experience, but can also be attributed to the continual non-duality at the heart of all forms. When encounters are assessed in this way, even the serial similarity that contributes to data recognition is subservient to immediate awareness.

But we need not limit our considerations to the egoic side of this equation. While the ego shares the experience of the form to be perceived, there is at the same time, a reciprocity that works in the other direction. When the ego performs the evaluation-expression function committed to it by the power continuum, the work is for the benefit of all aspects of that continuum and not merely for any particular egoic being. The ego is defined as a type of spokesman for the data of the universe and a full enactment of its function goes way beyond the advantage and appreciation of any individuated egoic construct. The wider and deeper view sees this complex used towards a growth of Self understanding within the wholeness of the power continuum.

But such an idea generally sounds strange to the ears of egoic man. The belief in separativity dominant in many beings today asserts an assumed dichotomy between objects and powers that might or might not influence them. Such a dualistic attitude nurtures the idea that the egoic form, in order to preserve itself, needs to guard and increase its present acquisitions whatever their form happens to be. Examples are formal knowledge, material goods or dependable relationships. Consequently, the popular idea of egoic pursuit concerns attempts to amass greater personal resources in order to increase the prospects for comfortable survival and success. The way in which this bias has arisen is the subject of our next chapter so is not enlarged on here, but the situation is stated as it so sharply contrasts the function that becomes apparent when we take a non-separatist view of man. Such a non-dualistic assessment is more acceptable both to logical analysis and the deeper sensory awareness rooted within a human being.

The two-way process that we noted earlier means that the egoic complex looks out to the perimeter that defines and distinguishes it from the rest of reality, and inward to find the intent that causes it to be. Alternatively, we could say that it looks inwards to discern the particular focus and outwards to scan the wholeness of the continuum in which this is clarified. Whichever way we like to consider it, and either is valid, the two-way observation is the creative tension that is fundamental to egoic function. All modalities of power can then be assessed from this dynamic focus. It clarifies the processes occurring within its particular form, the processes of other forms outside its integument, and the apparently formless forces that impinge on it. And always, the assessment is related to the stimulus received and the change evoked within the organism. In this way the ego is used to discern the characteristics of the macrocosm around it and the microcosm within its bounds.

All knowledge is therefore Self knowledge, and egoic function is concerned with the clarification of this fact. In the continuation of this chapter we will consider further the application of these principles in relation to the various aspects of human activity.

To an ordinary man the most readily apparent mode of experience is that of gross, substantial opposition. We have only to stub a toe on an unseen rock to be made painfully aware of this level of reality. But how does man define an interpretation of such basic haptic experience? Here we begin to see how the principles postulated earlier in this chapter are deduced from and referred back to direct practical encounters.

When our unwary walker stumbles on an unseen rock, he not only discerns a structure outside his skin, but a correspondent process operant within his own being. He may be highly unlikely to formulate such associations, but that need not detract from an awareness that supersedes empirical thought. Of course the rock outside feels hard and unyielding, but the assessment of this fact demands an inner interpretation as well as the outward encounter. And such interpretation involves the reciprocity to which we have referred. The outwardly directed attention seizes the object or situation and defines it according to the change or process perceived within the egoic being here operating to make the assessment. There is a relatively obvious corollary between the brittle hardness of the obstructive rock and the elastic rigidity of unyielding bone. We could therefore say that the egoic being is able to recognise the properties of hard, solid stone because within his integument he experiences a similar condensation of power operating to maintain his skeletal structure.

But we need not limit ourselves to such gross considerations of this process of assessment since other, more subtle factors, are also relevant. We have referred to the continuity of development, that is, the way in which every stage of evolution arises out of and incorporates those that precede it. Even a highly evolved egoic complex therefore includes data pertaining to the primal intensification of power that generates the mineral structure basic to the support of later emergents. Such rudimentary awareness can then contribute to the recognition of the properties of minerality by the egoic complex.

We have also noted that the serial presentation of the evolutionary phases depicts a process that is essentially immediate within the power continuum in every moment of existence. In other words, the intensification of power that generated the hard, slowly changing basis of creation, demonstrates a process that is still operant despite the apparent passing of that era. We cannot remind ourselves too often that the serial is an image of a dynamism that is eternal. Thus the objects created within the power continuum incorporate an awareness of that primal opposition and 'good grounding'. And it finds expression in the elastic hardness of bone. Thus the egoic complex knows serially and immediately the dynamic intensification of power that maintains the solidity of the offending rock.

But the assessment performed of this object need not be restricted to the features of stone. When egoic man evaluates its obdurate resistance, he can also begin to evaluate the processes operating to enable such an assessment. The impact with the rock generates the sensory flow and through reflection on this response the egoic man can increase his own self understanding. It is another instance of the two-way observation previously noted. The encounter occurs, the sensation is experienced and duly defined. The basis of such definition can then be evaluated and through it all egoic man can

46

seek progressive awareness of the causal factors that maintain the whole process. When this happens the egoic vehicle is being used to discern the interfunctioning modalities of awareness and thus begins to fulfil its role as an assessor.

The scope for such reflection by man and growth of self understanding, is not limited to physical encounters. Emotional experience can similarly become a means of progressive insight.

When we assess personal emotional responses it is probably less difficult to be aware of an inner and outer correspondence that underlies the evaluation. It is generally readily admitted that qualities such as joy or sorrow are discerned because beings have had similar experiences. When a person describes sorrow, joy or other named emotions occurring in friends, the assessment is based on the recall of similar sensations within his own experience. But this is only a superficial approach and highly vulnerable to sentiment or misinterpretation.

An approach more in keeping with our ontological analysis of encounter and assessment, is to remember that since all beings exist within a continuum, the emotion shown by one being is, at the same time, not limited to that person and not separate from the awareness of other beings. The interrelation of beings within the power continuum means that one person can actually share and recognise, but not identify with, the emotions of another being. It is another instance of assessing particular experience and data within the wholeness that allows it to be.

The two-way process fundamental to the self assessment of consciousness is founded upon the inherent sentience of the power continuum. We know what we know through a two-way exploration and interpretation due entirely to the inherent sensitivity of the continuum investing within its formal derivatives. This means that the education of egoic man is not some sort of indoctrination, or a process whereby he is given new knowledge previously alien to his being. Instead it is a leading out, or clarifying of understanding that is latent within him. It is new in its degree of clarity; it is not an acquisition previously absent and now appended. The two-way process distinguishes the possibilities that are already present, albeit hidden, within a sentient being. And they are sensed, known or experienced, only because of the inherent sentience that makes assessment possible. Thus when egoic man learns to discriminate and interpret what happens to him, this is due to the development and expression of an innate awareness rather than the acquisition of talents originally alien to his being.

The innate sensitivity of the power continuum involved in the egoic complex is therefore the basis of the explorations and assessments conducted through that zone. Whether the events assessed concern structures deemed 'outside' the being, or 'inside' its psyche, the assessment is due to the inherent sensitivity of formative power. If a man examines the head of a hammer, whether by deliberate inspection or by inadvertently striking his thumb with it, he evaluates a two-way sensory outflow and return. If he hears ideas expressed, whether they are in a precise, ordered presentation or a rambling political plea, he listens or turns away, accepts or rejects the data, in accordance with an inner sensitivity that acts as the primary assessor. Or if he joins an audience at a concert of music pleasant to his ears, a personal sensory awareness affords the basis of his assessments and interpretations of the performance and the reactions of those present. In any situation the innate sensitivity of power operant in the ego is the basic attribute that enables it first to locate itself and then express an assessment of the situation it meets. Such assessments are highly likely to be influenced, or even dominated, by the previously established preferences of the organism. But even so, it is still the inherent sentience of the receptive form that enables both the ordinary and finer evaluations to be made. This implies that all that is 'known' is due to the self discrimination of the sentient power continuum.

In the macrocosmic evolution, the plant era shows particularly clearly the compliance between the forms defined by the progressive differentiation within the power continuum, and the environmental forces distinguished as the 'elements' that influence them. In their ready response to environmental factors plants are clear tokens of the reciprocity between forces apparently 'inside' a defined zone and those 'outside' it. When the surroundings change, the plants adapt accordingly.

Egoic man can commonly show a similar process, despite possible attempts to restrain or civilise some of its manifestations. An inner sensory change provoking an outward emotive expression is often one of the first indications of man's reactions to his environment. The simple assessment 'I like it', or 'I dislike it', frequently has more influence on evaluations than allegedly 'unbiased' beings care to admit. Whether a person reacts with slight stiffening of the upper lip, a quiet sniff, or a loud laugh, his emotive equilibrium has changed first and the expression followed on. Such reactions of man to his environment echo the response of plants to forces that impinge on them and illustrate again the correspondence between activities of egoic man and features stressed in previous stages of evolution. It reiterates the point that serial development, whether macrocosmic or microcosmic, presents an unceasing dynamism that maintains egoic man and any object or situation he meets. It is the basic sensitivity shown with particular clarity by plants, that is no less essential to man and enables him to become aware of and express this aspect of being.

But such inherent ability, whilst it is fundamental to any process of evaluation, can also be applied by empirical man to his personal disadvantage and suffering. He may not only become aware of a particular event, but also focus on it so firmly that he over-identifies with it. And if that happens he becomes dominated by, and liable to suffer, its particular effects. This means that if an egoic being is given a present that pleases, or an insult that offends him/her, it is wiser to be aware of and assess the effects provoked, but not to fall into a separatist identification with them and consequent over-reliance on these effects.

The emotional problems so prevalent in recent decades are largely attributable to over-identification. If a man identifies exclusively with an egoic construct, of course he feels depressed by its failure and elated by its success. Whereas if he begins to see these as aspects of an evolutionary process which his egoic construct is designed by his hidden and higher Self to evaluate, a quality of interest hitherto unrealized begins to occur. Yet repeatedly, the separatist belief or over-identification gets in the way and leads man into the less useful and more painful attitude.

Most people do not want to behave like obdurate rocks. Of course we like the ability to perceive and express the feelings of our own or of other egoic beings. But it is to our advantage to pursue this in such a way that we do not fall into an exclusive identification with, and therefore reliance upon, an experience that is only a fragment of the dynamism that pertains to us. Feeling assessment is a primary mode of understanding, but we need to guard against its abuses, as well as develop its finer possibilities.

But it is not only the events around that are sensed and explored by the ego; the two-way process of observation and assessment is equally concerned with events operant within man. His inherent sentience is the rudiment by which he interprets processes internal to his being as well as those defined as outside his integument. Orientated in this way, the awareness invested in man progressively discerns his inner structuring, the data which can be known by accurate observation of personal reactions to peripheral events. So he watches for the response internal to his being as he meets differing situations and learns more of the processes operant within him.

But while some beings are eager to seek insight in this way, there are others who prefer to turn a 'blind eye' to inner structuring. Many people prefer not to discuss it and even try to deny its effect on their actions. But even when such barriers are erected, personal inner processes are prone to break through, perhaps in unpleasant dreams, or increasingly in recent decades, in psychological symptoms that are beyond man's empirical control.

Such disturbance is not the only way in which man is challenged to consider his 'psyche'. An increasing number of beings are finding that the innate awareness, that we have referred to as inherent sentience, provokes a discontent with interpretations of life that do not pay adequate heed to its presence. Because egoic man is posited within the sentient continuum, he can never be totally excluded from any aspect of it. So although he may at times appear to stress relatively defined, material constructs, he can never completely forget their correspondents within his psyche.

Thus it is the sentience invested within egoic man that both provokes the search for self understanding and enables the expression

50

of relevant data. When man formulates terms for what he finds, it is to convey the processes that he first senses to be operant. Hence the terms used to clarify the awareness of the dynamism operant in man, are only made possible because of the sentience that is prior to any formulation.

But the evaluatory function performed through the egoic complex is not limited to the assessment of constructs in the world around it, or to the inner world often described as its 'own'. Again it is the sentience inherent to the ego that senses there is further to go, that phenomenological data are not a complete explanation of life experience. In other words, it is aware of aspects of conscious activity that defy formal analysis.

At this point we are returning to the consideration of the creative intent evidenced by the ego itself and the forms it is designed to evaluate. And it is the primal sentience of the continuum, invested in the ego through involution that gradually draws us towards such appraisal. It is an expression of the intent to look, not only at the phenomena defined, but also through or within them towards a heightened awareness of an aspect of power that initiates and controls its manifestations.

Nothing happens without a cause. Logic, as well as sentience, reminds us of this fact, and therefore of the need to look, not only for the form posited, but for the intent that allows it to be. But logic is a formative process and, as intentionality is immediate, it is beyond its linear definitions. The form of the act is seen, but not the decision to perform it. If I sit on a chair, my posture, whether upright or slouching, can be seen and assessed. The form of the act is readily evident and expresses my decision to behave in that way. But the decision itself is never seen. In any activity we see the effects of a decision rather than the impulse of the decision itself.

The impulse of a decision is immediate to every moment in which an act is performed. When I sit on a chair the intent is immediate; that is, it is the choice of every moment of sitting. The intent may, of course, appear to repeat itself and present as non-different from one second to another. But even such apparent serial repetition is maintained by an immediate decision. The momentary choice, or orientation of the will, is operant even though it is commonly

51

veiled by serial sequence. Intentionality always goes beyond linear repetition. It therefore follows that when we begin to consider the creative intent we are moving through the limits set by definition towards new modes of consciousness.

But in order to define anything, a limit or perimeter, is set. Without such it would not be defined. Consciousness therefore establishes a boundary within itself, that is, a known pattern that may be repeated. But such repetition, if it was assumed to be no more than repetitive, would be a direct contradiction of the immediacy operant in a 'now' moment. The essence of such a moment, which Kierkegaard calls an 'instant', is that it operates as it will in this immediate point. Therefore, although consciousness may define a boundary within itself, it is a definition made in and for this moment. Thus it is an affirmation of its activity <u>now</u>, and not conformity to a previously established path.

In other words, when we refer to the immediacy that transcends definition, we mean that it transcends serial repetition of definition. Of course it uses terms for reference, but such terms are being constantly redefined and reapplied. It is an active use of terminology consciously applied in the moment, and not a passive adherence to modes of practice which largely forget the will or intent now operant within them.

But how do we become more aware of such dynamic intentionality? Again, it is by the sentience invested within us. If we return to the illustration of sitting on a chair we can say it is our inner sensitivity which makes us aware of our decision to do it, whether it is because of a 'free' choice or an order we have decided to obey. It is by means of the sentience inherent to form that we may become increasingly aware of the intent that directs its actions. And thus it is by the refining of sensitivity that we gain further insight into creative intentionality. In this way we are continually rediscovering the essential contribution to our evolution occurring through the egoic complex.

Arising out of the insights that sentience thus affords we may begin to formulate expressions related to the creative intentionality that the ego is designed to observe. We can say that the intent is in no way separate from, or alien to, any process of power. The intent is the intent of the power, and the power is the power of the intent. Problems arise when this non-duality is forgotten. But the sentience vested within the egoic complex can be the means of its rediscovery.

This brings us again to the idea of the two-way process. The sentient ability of power enables us to feel outwards to the form defined, and inwards to the defining intent. It is like a two-edged sword. While the more refined levels of sentience are reaching towards the creative intent, the less refined aspects, attracted by pleasure pursuit and pain avoidance, can easily identify with the forms that seem most likely to provoke the sensations that are sought. The sentience vested within the egoic zone can thus be orientated outwardly towards a reliance on formalised processes, or inwardly towards rediscovery of the awareness of the causal intent. And the egoic consciousness can become the means of investigating its own possibilities as well as those of the forms outside its bounds.

Thus it is through the ego complex that we experience and clarify the contrasting sensations associated with empirical reliance on formal constructs on one hand, and movement towards rediscovery of intentionality on the other. Used in this way to discern the aspects of consciousness operant in and through it, the ego becomes a means of increasing Self realization.

Although the awareness of intentionality may be suppressed in man for long periods of time, it can never be absolutely alienated from his being. Even the most determined empiricist knows that his understanding of a functional unit cannot be complete if the force that directs it remains obscure. Such awareness can become a major contributor to the recurrent restlessness of man, provoking him always to look for insights, new degrees of comprehension. In due course such research passes through the over emphasis on formal constructs so that instead of seeking only, or predominantly, for more empirical data to append to the egoic self, man begins to look for the awareness of the causal intent, the causal power that he knows to be fundamental to any functional unit. In this way the sentience vested within man leads him to look both towards and beyond the defining data he is used to express.

At this point we will briefly digress to consider the possible relevance of these insights to the 'battle of the sexes'. Every being, because it is formed by and within the power continuum, is not divorced from any aspect of that continuum. But at the same time, there are obviously apparent differences due to stress in differing beings on various aspects of behaviour. In general we can see a widespread tendency for men to place particular stress on formalising and women on sensitivity. This does not imply that men cannot be emotive or women rational, it is merely stating a direction of relative stress commonly exhibited. As a result of this a male partner will often make a formal analysis of a situation and expect this to be regarded as adequate. Meanwhile, the female partner will often sense innuendoes and implications too subtle for spoken expression and perhaps refute the assumed adequacy of the male analysis. This situation can easily become a cause of friction that proves useful if it provokes the male, not only to make a more accurate definition of events, but also to begin to respect the sentience, the subtle sensitivity, shown by his partner. While the woman in the situation may similarly be induced to define more appropriately the factors that she 'senses' to be relevant. When this happens the friction engendered can provoke increased understanding of the interaction in both partners.

This type of 'battle' is not restricted to the interactions between existential beings defined as 'men' and 'women'. This outward, ordinarily visible situation is also an image of the polarisation of power within every being. The interplay between a rational formulating ability and the sensitivity that both uses and transcends it, is continually transacted in being. It is by such internal self opposition that we may realize progressively finer qualities of the sentience involved in being and the referential terms that it posits. Thus an egoic being learns increasingly to respect the function of definition as a vehicle for the sentience that transcends as well as sustains it, whether that definition relates to the terms he uses or to the formal aspect of power usually referred to as his bodily 'self'. It can therefore lead to a greater self respect based on insight into the function for which the 'lower' self is designed by the hidden and 'higher' Self. Or to put it another way, it is a growing realization that the ordinary experiential vehicle readily identified as 'self', although merely an aspect of being rather than its entirety, is a means of rediscovering the modes of consciousness that are ever present but often forgotten or ignored by man.

54

Each glimpse into finer levels of awareness enables a greater comprehension of the function served by the egoic form and therefore enhances its use towards a further growth of consciousness. Thus the insight into the function of formulation can become a self propagating process and the egoic vehicle, by virtue of the sentience vested within it, may increasingly realize the value of the defining function it is designed to serve. In this way it learns an authentic respect for its 'self' and the data it is enabled to evaluate.

The finer possibilities of sentience, to which we have referred earlier in this chapter, are the means of such progressive realization. It may be described as an awareness of awareness, or a greater insight into the levels of consciousness operant in being. This is the essence of egoic function. We have previously deduced that the ego complex is primarily concerned with the Self disclosure of creative power. Thus it is through the co-operation of highly refined sensitivity and Self structuring of power, with each of these aspects serving as a mirror to the other, that greater Self understanding is realized.

Such heightened awareness in turn leads to a re-evaluation of the defining capability shown by the egoic complex, and immediately highlights the contrast between this developing insight and inertic, empirically based ideas.

It is not uncommon for such stress to be placed on man's part in the evolutionary process that the wider view is obscured. At the same time the belief is usually nurtured that man alone has learnt to name and use phenomena such as the raw materials of the earth, the flora and fauna they support, or the atomic forces they contain. Consequently it is a popular idea that egoic man, by virtue of 'his' empirical experience and 'his' superior intelligence, is able to order and manipulate at least some of the forms around him.

But when the deeper levels of sentience operant within us stir the remembrance that man, like all other functional complexes, is a process of power maintained within the original power continuum, we begin to make a very different assessment of the defining activity performed. The ability shown by man in describing and using forms around him is due, not to a separate empirically-self-activated egoic unit learning to do such things, but to the fact that the primal continuum adapts man to function in this way. When reality is assessed in this manner we can say that the formulating and technical skills of man exist because the continuum enables them to operate, and not because of man's assumed intelligence and other acquired characteristics.

Neither can we say that even if man originates in the continuum, he then exclusively maintains and pursues his 'own' course. Perhaps separatist man would like to think in this way, but the suggestion does not stand up to ontological analysis. The concept of the continuum is permanently applicable, whether or not man remembers it. The defining ability shown by man is invested in him by that continuum at all times. It is a function performed within the power field for the benefit of all and not merely a process whereby egoic man learns to name and appropriate forms to his empirical use.

If ordinary man likes, for a time, to regard his activity as his 'own' prowess to be developed for his 'own' ends, that is indeed his 'own' business. But it does not hinder the wider view, and does not prevent the defining function of man from being performed for the service of the whole power field.

So what is achieved by definition? Its use for clarifying a stable reference is obvious. When the referential edge of any form is clear it can be recognised and used. Increasingly precise definition is essential to a corresponding increase of understanding of function. Definition sets the limits within which the processes of power characteristic of a particular form can be seen and assessed. Thus formulation and apparent separation are the means of differentiating and recognising the attributes of the original power continuum and supremely the causal intent that maintains the stable reference.

We have recurrently considered that the ego learns of this process by self involvement in it. Thus, in order to define, it is itself defined, and the definition of its bounds enables it to recognise and express the data of events that concern it. In this way the ego is invested with the function of evaluation and expression of the realities of life. It serves as a focal point, defined with sufficient clarity to enable it to experience, recognise and disclose different modes of action. Or, in colloquial terms, it can both see and be seen.

This brings us to the correlation of the egoic expressive function and the faculty of speech. An ability to speak is clearly of cardinal importance for the pursuit of egoic function. It is sometimes asserted that speech appears in conjunction with the evolution of the cerebral hemispheres in man. We know that these two events concur but this is not the whole explanation of the development of speech.

When we consider that speech is a function of being clarified within the power continuum, we can see that, like the emergent ego, it occurs when there is a crucial balance between firm definition of and by power yet sufficient relaxation to enable expression of its data. The expression of speech requires the interplay of mechanical fixation and movements. We see this in the opposition between free airflow from the lungs, and impeding vocal structures in the larynx, that between them produce sounds with at least some degree of clarity.

A similar opposing interplay occurs between other mechanisms that secure and mobilise vocal structures, and within the mental sphere where there has to be sufficient agility to compare related concepts yet sufficient clarity to verbalise one at a time. Thus in both the mechanical and mental realms of experience there is a balance between fixation and relaxation that enables speech. Which means that yet again we have an illustration of the self opposition of power that is basic to any manifestation of its attributes.

The expression of insight now possible through this interaction is essential to pursuit of the egoic function. But let it be emphasised that this process is worked out through the egoic zone as a function of the whole power continuum. It is not merely the effort of the form defined to such a degree that it is now able to distinguish its 'self' and events that concern it. For a time a superficial analysis may support the idea that man alone assesses, names and utilises the forms he meets. But closer inspection uncovers the interfunction that is always present.

Insight into egoic function is an accompaniment to the clarification of its dynamic form. The prior stages in its evolution are continually leading up it, and the new understanding of its functional possibilities further enhances its role.

Such clarification not only enables present data to be seen for what they are, but leads on to the elaboration of new modes of application. That is, we not only see more clearly steps that contribute to present functional commitments, but discover new ways to apply them. Using a camera or a computer can rapidly remind us that the greater our understanding of them, the more we can enjoy using them. A similar principle applies in relation to egoic function. Heightened understanding of the data defined with egoic zeal can enhance personal function and enjoyment.

There are a vast number of illustrations that we could consider here. Not least is the correlation between speech and intellectual clarification worked out through the ego. We referred to this interaction earlier in this chapter, and return to it now as it is again relevant at this stage in our discussion.

All of us will be aware of the value of clear, concise words and the contrast when they are slurred or lost. This point is very clearly expressed in one of the books by Stanislavski, founder of the Moscow Art Theatre. His book 'Building a Character' describes the training of drama students seen through the eyes of a particular pupil, Kostya. When he recounts the tuition in 'Diction and Singing' Kostya quotes the words of the director Tortsov who says to his pupils

'Think how much is packed into a word or phrase, how rich language is. It is powerful, not in itself but inasmuch as it conveys the human soul, the human mind .... sounds convey words, words phrases, phrases thoughts, and out of thoughts there are formed whole scenes....a great play that embraces the tragic life of a human soul...These sounds form a whole symphony!' And in contrast, Tortsov thus describes the effect of distorted words

'Poor speech creates one misunderstanding after another. It clutters up, befogs, or even conceals the thought, the essence of the play.'

It is also interesting to note in these paragraphs how Stanislavski reiterates, through the person of Tortsov, a point to which we have referred recurrently in this study. He says:

'Letters, syllables, words were not invented by man, they were suggested to him by his instincts, impulses, by nature herself, time and place.'

Whilst these quotations emphasise the interrelation and importance of form and function, they also hint at the power behind it. As always, precise clarification of the form expressed similarly reveals its function and indicates the power modalities involved in the process.

Whether it is the opposition that generates its substance, the limitation that sets its perimeter, the sensation that evaluates any aspect of it, or supremely the intent that maintains it, all these are known through reference to the edge that distinguishes the form. Thus through the clarification of particular forms within the power continuum we may discover, as well as the features of that form, a resonance or harmony of interfunctioning modalities of the power that maintains it.

The 'symphony' formed by sounds is presented in three ways.

The first and generally most obvious one is the flow of an orderly series of distinct notes that together constitute a melodic line. The second one is the harmony within a musical chord, itself a blending of distinct tones. The third mode is more subtle and is found in the components of each single note. It is a harmony constituted by the resonance of the processes that lead into and beyond every individual note. Each sound can be likened to an hour glass, with the note formed being the central constriction while before it the power focuses into clarity and beyond it reaches to new levels of awareness.

This effect may be compared to egoic processes. Like a defined note, the ego is posited to express more than the limits of its defined form. When the blinds of empirical separatist belief are drawn back, and we begin to glimpse the wider and deeper aspects of the power within us, it is possible to sense the 'symphony' of sound co-operant in each note of egoic identification. The ego, like the single sound, is continually maintained by harmonics or aspects of consciousness often unnoticed by a casual listener. But in the performance of its function the ego may learn to listen and thereby become increasingly aware of the dynamism that maintains it and enables its range of manifestations.

So what can we now say of the new insights into power being found through the egoic operation? First we may refer to a greater understanding of the processes that lead to the formation and function of the ego, or of any form evaluated by it. Next, and arising out of this, we may discuss the way in which the egoic zone is made increasingly aware that it need not be as empirically biased as it usually appears. Thus we gradually realize that the ego complex, and the forms it is designed to evaluate, are likewise dynamic aspects of the sentient power continuum in which all processes interfunction. We could say that the movement of the clearly defined, divisive structure is the progressive clarification of possibilities glimpsed in chaos. And that through the constriction we move into a stage of comprehensive integrated reorganisation as the clear focus won is set in relation to the whole continuum. Considered in this way, the ego is seen as an intermediary between confused chaos and conscious re-synthesis.

In the course of this process it is probable that for a time the egoic zone will feel relatively isolated. But this does not have to happen. The mode of its occurrence, and how it can be overcome, are subjects of later chapters. The clarification and expression of data for which the egoic zone is designed can be performed while the awareness is retained of the source, or 'symphony', in which that note originates.

Thus, through the particular we move into an increasingly comprehensive view of reality. Such a view, or experience of power, is more than a summation of the prior stages. We can use the analogy of mixing colours to illustrate this point. If we mix yellow and blue pigments we do not see only an alternation of these colours but a new quality, green. A similar principle applies here. When the aspects of power that contribute to the clarity found through the ego are integrated, the operative consciousness disclosed is more than the summation of the prior stages of awareness. It is a new insight that is both sharper and more sensitive than that previously known. Famous mystics have likened it to a sense of immanence, an awareness of all that is focused in this point of reference. The Hindu philosophy of Shankara Charya describes it as 'Advaita', the non-duality, the not-twoness of all things. The master of Zen, or a Samurai swordsman trained in this tradition, and immediately conscious of the dynamic possibilities of a situation, are able to respond instantly to an opponent's attack.

There is a marked contrast between such highly refined sensitivity, and that ordinarily known to empirical beings reliant on their five senses. The comparison highlights the restraint and inhibition in the empirical reliance and the quick, alert beauty in comprehensive awareness. The egoic function is concerned with the inner experience of defining limits in contrast to which is appreciated the unthinkably quick appraisal of comprehensive consciousness.

We have now considered four modes of awareness that the egoic unit is designed to evaluate. Each of these has its own type of movement with its own characteristics. We have seen that the first, and generally more obvious level, is that of physical obstruction evidenced particularly by the structures of the mineral world and the earth's crust. After this we have the plant era where we see the flow of rhythmic response but in complete harmony with the universal force and not yet sufficiently differentiated to uproot and pursue its 'own' ends. After this we come to the animal era, which in its more developed phase becomes egoic man. Here the constituent rhythm has sufficiently demarcated and distinguished a form for it to be able to pursue separatist aims not necessarily in accordance with the environmental flux. The fourth stage, that we have called comprehensive awareness, is the rhythmic flow that, not only performs and knows its differentiated action, but also begins to understand its co-operation with previously forgotten aspects of the power continuum. This is therefore where the egoic zone begins to function in a new way; it now affirms its particular limits and associated behavioural differences, but in the simultaneous awareness of its true significance. In other words, it knows the particular focus but within the wholeness of the power that posits it.

At this point it realizes that all function is interfunction, not only in the sense of defined forms interacting in a co-ordinated manner, but that in each unique focus there is an interfunction of modalities of power convergent on that point. Describing this in geometric terms we could say that the awareness is spherical rather than linear. It is a recognition that the continuity of power refers to the unceasing interaction of all modalities of power and its apparently diverse forms.

61

It realizes therefore, that interfunction refers to the immediate convergence of the differentiated levels of power that together constitute an observant being. We may call this the comprehensive phase.

Each of these four stages, although they may be likened to particular forms or structures, has its own characteristic sensations. And they are known most clearly by recognition of those sensations. The forms of words associated with them are vehicles to imply or convey the awareness, but essentially knowledge of the stages is by sensory recognition rather than by formal analysis. Here again, it is opposition Self established within the containing sentient power continuum, that enables the evaluation of the sensory data.

Considered in this way evolution can be considered as a progressive discrimination and appreciation of sentience. We have noted before that the original power continuum is sentient. Thus to discern sensory modalities is to discern power. To dichotomise the form of power and a sensation it might or might not afford is a hangover of erroneous 19th century dualism. Sensation is not an optional extra sometimes evoked by power; it is power. And to distinguish sensation is to distinguish power. The slow, obdurate resistance of minerality; the compliant, yielding flux of vegetation;, the quickening separatist pursuit of empirical man; and the unthinkably quick comprehension that scans all these and more besides; are aspects of the sentient power discerned according to their sensory qualities. It is all too easy to assume that sentience is simply for the understanding of formal constructs. But what we are saying here is that the equation is at least as valid the other way round and that the formative processes exhibited are a means of discerning the sentience of the power continuum.

We have said that the comprehensive awareness scans the levels of consciousness that precede it 'and more besides'. What do we mean by this? Here we are approaching a fifth level of awareness, the quintessence, or the controlling intent to which we have previously referred.

At the beginning of our study of egoic function we deduced that it is concerned with 'dynamic intentionality'. Following on from this we have considered the way in which the differing aspects or modes of that dynamism express the initiating power and its creative intent. Awareness of such intentionality is the quintessence of consciousness. We may refer to it as the essence of control, the will, or the higher Self. Terms such as these are used to indicate an immediacy of full control too quick to be recounted fully by any linear form of words. In geometric symbols we may liken it to the point at the centre of a circle. It is an awareness so fine that it is referred to as 'immediate' and known only to itself in the moment of operation. To describe it further, terms have been used such as 'instantaneous' and 'unconditional imperative'. It is an imperative now in the sense that it is the controlling intent of a 'now' moment, yet simultaneously it is unconditioned, able to act as it will and answerable to none other than itself.

In the course of evolution we may begin to glimpse such levels of awareness, with logic or intuition aiding the disclosure. And we can imagine that a being enabled to fully attain and co-operate with such levels of consciousness would be truly Self controlled, the word Self here referring to the creative power operant within the referential being. If we further deduce the implications of the fact of the continuum, we can say that such a being would be acting in harmony with the universal flux, which he affirms to be not other than himself. Thus he would understand and control the interfunctioning aspects of the power within his integument, and their relation to the forces and events that impinge on him.

The full enactment of such a possibility may be very rarely seen, but that need not deter us from considering it. And as we do so, we may find glimpses of insight that gradually enable us to seek the awareness hidden within our own being. The developmental path will be unique to each person, but in sundry ways we may begin to consider and even realize the possibilities of the consciousness operant within us. Such rediscovery is the essence of egoic function.

Thus the ego serves as a channel though which insight may be gained into the forces that constitute it. The evaluation performed is through direct self experience of the modalities described. In this way the ego becomes a means of progressive understanding or insight into the forces operating within and around it. And as such comprehension develops there is further re-evaluation of the egoic function in relation to it.

Yet again it is a two-way process. The ego serves as a focal channel to enhance the understanding of the power that constitutes it. At the same time the insight into the aspects of power enables greater awareness of and co-operation with, the egoic function.

Thus through the reciprocal advancement there can be a progressive disclosure of consciousness approaching a point where the true immediacy of power, and function of the ego in its discovery, may be realized. At that stage the ego will be seen in a new light and its true function begin.

Here we are anticipating later chapters of this study.

Although the egoic zone may temporarily forget the five-fold immediacy of power, it remains a focus through which the evaluation process continues. Man may forget, but the Absolute does not. Even though man may be relatively unaware of the processes operating in and through him, they continue to run their course according to the Absolute intent. Therefore within the power continuum the egoic complex is always a vehicle for the evaluation and assessment of modalities of power. And in due course man may become more aware of, and learn to co-operate with, the five-fold inter-function of his consciousness.

Until that state is attained it is man who suffers the lack of control, insight, or interest regarding the events within or around him. Forgetfulness of the five-fold immediate interfunction is at the basis of the sufferings of egoic man.

Such a consideration may lead us to question why or how empirical beings become so preoccupied with lesser degrees of awareness and often seem to prefer to forget the dynamic intentionality operating within them.

This brings us to our next chapter, the fixation of the ego.

Chapter 5: The Fixation of the Ego

We are using the term 'fixation' here to refer to the process through which the egoic experience becomes limited temporarily to the empirical data derived in a particular life span. It indicates a reliance on the facts that egoically identified man assumes he has himself proved, or accepted as proved by other men. It is therefore another way of describing the bias of consciousness to the apparent form it defines concurrent with disregard of the dynamism maintaining it. Or using the terminology applied in Chapter 3, it is the development of the 'empirical ego'.

The photographic process involving the use of film aptly illustrates the idea considered here. Before the exposed film is immersed in the fixative solution it is handled with great care and due respect paid to the subsequent steps required for printing. But once fixed, the picture rather than the method of its production, generally becomes the main focus of attention. A similar shift of attention occurs with egoic fixation. The purpose of this chapter of our study is to consider the steps through which this change occurs within the egoic structure.

We have previously noted that such fixation does not have to occur, that empirical reliance is not an unavoidable concomitant of egoic function. But its development is the usual experience of man and increased understanding of the steps involved will in due course contribute to the eventual fulfilment of its role when the 'fixation' will be re-assessed and released.

This line of study is itself an application of the egoic function. We have been considering the use of the ego in the self assessment of creative power. A similar purpose applies to a review of the fixation process. To assess the way in which the egoic awareness becomes restricted to an empirical bias can afford further insights into the behavioural possibilities of the power continuum. Thus a greater understanding of the changes associated with egoic fixation itself supports the revelatory intent. It is not only that we seek to comprehend fixation in order to know how it may be rectified. The insight into the process, as well as the release of consciousness with which it may be associated, together support the revelatory function of the power continuum.

But before we begin a more detailed look at the phenomenology of the steps in egoic fixation, let us emphasise again that even though we may appear to be describing linear changes, they always imply dynamics operant in every moment of existence. It will be a great help to our studies if this point can be born in mind. The steps to be considered in the process that we are calling egoic fixation are not merely linear; they are immediate to every moment in which such fixation occurs. In other words, the changes do not start with the year dot and culminate in a ripe old age. The steps of the primary inclination and pursuit of egoic demands operate in every moment of its fixation and, let it be added, are similarly reversible.

So how does this fixation occur? We will start our consideration by clarifying a negative aspect. That is, by reminding ourselves that it is not an unavoidable result of egoic formation. We noted in an earlier chapter that all created forms are posited by the in-holding of the power continuum; that power acting in compliance with its own intent in-holds to such a degree that it generates apparently discrete, substantial forms. But the operations that distinguish the egoic form need not necessarily be associated with the limitation of consciousness that is implied by the word 'fixation' in its present usage. That is, the clarification of the form within the sentient field does not have to be accompanied by the fixation of awareness.

We can use our hands to illustrate this point. When we look at a hand it is possible to focus on part of it, the index finger for example, to such a degree that the rest of the hand appears blurred and may be ignored. But if we take a wider view and see the structure as a whole, it is possible to make an immediate assessment of both the differentiation and interfunction of the various parts. In this way we may clarify which parts are the most nimble, strong or sensitive, and at the same time retain an awareness that each member, though distinct, is supported by the whole complex in which the diverse features co-operate. Thus the awareness of clarity and interfunction can be co-existent.

The same principle applies to the ego. It is possible for its distinctive features and functions to be clarified while at the same time the awareness is retained of the dynamic continuum within which it is defined. Thus differentiation is not necessarily the cause of fixation and limitation. Or in other words, the 'ego' does not have to become the 'empirical ego'.

But although egoic fixation does not have to develop, it generally does so and we will now consider how this occurs.

We have seen that the ego is defined as an individuated complex through which the attributes of the power continuum are evaluated. But in this process there is an obvious and inherent danger. The definition of the ego incurs the risk that the zone now distinguished will over stress its 'own' status, assume that 'it' as an individual unit is operating as a stand alone structure and forget its unceasing reliance on the power continuum. The bias of consciousness, that we are here calling the 'fixation' of the ego, develops when there is sufficient superstress on a particular formal presentation within the power continuum together with forgetting, or wilful disregard, of the other power modalities co-operant with it.

The next step in tracing the path that leads to such fixation is therefore to look at the factors that influence the stress and superstress on the formal aspect of the ego. We may find it helpful here to let our creative imagination scan appropriately the vectors operating prior to and during egoic fixation.

Prior to the differentiation of distinct forms we cannot say that there is no awareness of what is happening, only that it is not clarified and assessed in the manner usually associated with knowledge and understanding. We may intuit that the awareness at this stage is present but confused, not distinguished, a state of apparent chaos. It is like someone who 'senses' that something is happening but cannot say how or why she knows it. And we can say further of such awareness that, because it is associated with a stage prior to formulation where the apparent division of field power is unknown, that its attributes are shared throughout itself without dissension. The aspects of power, which in due course are to be experienced as selective authority and awareness, are therefore at this stage immediate to the whole power field. It is such diffuse or shared awareness and authority which we describe as 'pre-egoic' and which the empirical ego attempts to usurp.

But while the differentiation of form makes possible such a changing sense of authority, other inherent aspects of the formative power similarly attain a new intensity. That is, through the relative stress associated with a new application of power, its authority and other attributes simultaneously find new degrees of expression.

Studies of the early stages of developing life forms have shown the prominent effects of pleasure/pain vectors. In fact, their influence is arguably sufficient to warrant their description as a primal protopathic urge. We see evidence of them in any emergent life form; the amoeba avoiding a noxious stimulus, the plant inclining towards light and warmth, an animal retreating from threat and a child demanding food, all illustrate this basic drive. As our study continues we will consider in progressive detail its contribution to egoic development.

The original movement of power to generate the ego implies a response to an initiative immediately applicable to each and all of its inherent modalities. That is, it moves, not only to formulate and build up the egoic complex, but also in order to satisfy itself within its own terms of pleasure/pain and other modes of self discovery. Thus the progressive intensification of power that clarifies the structure of the ego also clarifies the sensation of pleasure/pain. Differentiation of one aspect of the power continuum implies differentiation of all its attributes. Through the intensification that heightens the perception of form, the awareness of pleasure/pain, authority and any other modality of primal power is similarly increased.

At this stage we may note a potential hazard. Pleasure and pain are two words used so often that we could easily assume a wider understanding of their implications than closer examination would support. So to aid our discussion at this stage let us take another look at their implications.

We know from personal experience that an energy input that commonly affords a sensation we call pleasure will give pain if intensified beyond a certain point. For instance, the warmth and glow of a brightly burning fire are welcome on a dark December day. But if a hand is placed too near to it, that same fire becomes a source of pain and possibly terror. The same principle applies with sound stimuli, which at appropriate levels for an individual recipient can be pleasant and acceptable, whereas if they are distorted or excessively intensified, they can become painful and repellent. These basic examples, taken from the many that could be cited, illustrate that a personal ability to receive and assimilate a stimulus is a key factor in determining whether its impact is assessed and described as 'pleasant' or 'painful', and therefore likely to be accepted or rejected by the recipient.

Because it accords with the structure of the recipient, an energy input experienced as pleasure can usually be readily assimilated. But in contrast, the input that cannot be accommodated in this way and is not aligned to the egoic structure will feed into sub-cortical or sub-egoic data. That is, a pleasant experience is integrated by the recipient organism and is liable to be retained from its initial impact as a relatively enduring integrated record within its substance. But with painful stimuli a very different effect is seen. Here the original energy input is other than the organism can assimilate with the result that its modalities are not adequately balanced. Hence they are retained in a state of discord where the unclarified emotive aspects are sensed but not aligned with relevant forms. In this way the being acquires an experiential record which has not been fully assessed on receipt. But data are then present which may be reinvestigated and re-aligned by the individual recipient at a later stage, perhaps through an appropriate use of psychotherapy, when sub-egoic data relating to pain can be re-examined and brought into conscious integration. But in contrast to this, pleasure imprints, because they are more readily integrated when received by an individual person, are less amenable to this type of modification.

An example may help to clarify this contrast. A child who enjoys a peaceful picnic will assimilate the relevant data. But a child in a similar situation and disturbed by a swarm of bees, even if he is not stung by the bees, is likely to be severely frightened. As a result he is unlikely to integrate the energy input and may retain a fear not only of bees, but also of picnics or other similar adventures. In this instance the stimuli and their effects are likely to be too rapid for adequate assessment and assimilation, and will set up within the organism unclarified sensory impressions. In order to re-align such imprints the individual could later re-examine the event, re-evaluate its components and perhaps release emotions not expressed during the initial experience. He could then recognise that the fears provoked were attributable to bees rather than picnics or similar outings. In this way he could be freed from misinterpretations that could otherwise prejudice his assessments and limit his activities. In this way a previously painful experience can be re-evaluated and the individual person concerned, whilst releasing from potential restrictions on future activity, can also increase his personal insight.

So what can we now say concerning the pleasure/pain vectors? We have noted the prominence of their effects in emergent life forms. Such reactions are rudimentary and universal, contributing to the development of every living organism. They are a major factor in the response we described in Chapter 3 as 'the pleasure in the edge', a reaction that inclines the newly emergent form not only to accept its definition, but also to start to identify with it. We can deduce now that such a pleasurable reaction is a new quality made possible in the instant in which the new definition is achieved. It is not an experience of pleasure previously known and now focused on a new-found form; it is an awareness of pleasure discrimination unique to the newly perceived form. It is not like someone who has known a particular quality of pleasure finding another form to produce a similar effect; the pleasure and the form are both at once new found sensations.

To some people this may sound a trivial point and they may question why it is being emphasised here. It is given such emphasis at this point in our study because it is one of the basic processes that contribute to the fixation of egoic awareness on empirical data. These early steps may seem so slight that some people would regard them as insignificant. But their importance is realized when we begin to see how they support the initial movement towards changes of increasing magnitude. It is possible to be so fascinated by the preliminary experience of new pleasure modalities that the awareness of other aspects of the power continuum is temporarily suppressed. Where this happens the egoic complex becomes a trap, and for the time being inhibits rather than enhances its insight into the dynamism maintaining it.

The new found quality of delight operates as a primary vector in this process. It gradually attracts the focus of consciousness to the pleasure found through the form now being defined, with the result that the particular operational limits are progressively affirmed while the constituent power is forgotten. The ego then believes increasingly that 'it' as an individuated unit performs its activity, and attempts to deny the whole creative cycle.

We see an example of this in a developing child. In the first few months the primal protopathic urge vested within the infant strongly expresses itself. Consequently the vocal and other modes of demand are readily apparent. But although at this stage the child can let such wants be known, it can do relatively little towards meeting them by its 'own' efforts. It is dependent on the parental figures for food, protection etc., and knows it. But with the impaction of energy into its form it becomes increasingly able to move and assert itself, and usually joyfully exhibits this to people around. We therefore see children delighting to display their deeds, whether it is marks made as fingers trace through food on a plate, an ability to walk, or excreta passed into a pot and proudly placed before approving adults. The child, whilst proving such abilities to himself, presents his newly found prowess for others to admire. And as he does so, his pleasure is usually readily evident.

But when the child focuses on particular actions in this way, he is intensifying, not only his delight, but also the changing sense of authority. This means that the sense of self assertion and pleasure, increasing together, conspire to attract progressive focus by the child onto its defined locus. Thus the child showing what it can do is likely simultaneously to believe that he, as a separate unit, is doing it. As a result the reliance on empirical processes grows and the awareness of interfunction diminishes. And a child, whilst increasing its awareness of its egoic reference, may become progressively confined to its empirical data.

The key to this sequence is the fascination by the newly found pleasure and apparent authority. And once established, such a process tends to operate in a self propagating circle. The pleasure discrimination intensifies the focus on the form, this reinforces the

71

clarity of that formal perception and with it the pleasurable quality is made yet keener. The focus is then further intensified, again increasing the perception of pleasure, and so on.

The experience of pleasure in apparent success, or assuming we have proved we can perform some particular act, is well known to all of us whatever our age. It commonly affords an example of this cyclical process. The power operating as egoic man, usually enjoys the apparent proof of its capabilities. Here again, the sense of pleasure experienced as the constituent power utilises the defined channel, reinforces the egoic identification.

Whether we consider the process as exemplified by a child or adult, or assess it in the more general terms of ontology, it comes back to a similar sequence of fascination by pleasure associated with apparent prowess, and resultant shift of awareness towards increasing formal reliance. Thus the pleasure bias within the primal protopathic field proves instrumental in the fixation of consciousness onto empirical data.

But let it again be emphasised that such a pursuit of the pleasure bias is only one of the modalities operant within primal power. This process is but one of many possibilities and although it is commonly seen, it does not have to occur. That is, it is not the only course that can be enacted within the evolving power forms and although it frequently happens, it is not an inevitable occurrence.

If we apply the language of theology at this point, we could describe this process of fixation of consciousness as the 'fall'. This term is used to refer to the change that occurs as the previously unrestricted awareness of the power continuum so focuses that it 'falls' into reliance upon, and limitation by, a particular form. If we take an ontological look at the Genesis account of the Eden story and Adam's fall, we find an exact analysis of the process operating in egoic fixation.

The garden can be seen as representing the power continuum with its inherent possibilities, and Eve the sensitivity of that power, now appearing as a woman and able to be distracted by the fruit produced. So we read that in response to the serpentine whisper, she 'saw that the tree was good for food ... pleasant to the eyes ... and ... to be desired to make one wise'. She then ate of the fruit herself, and gave some to Adam. If we see Eve as a symbol of the primal sensitivity, and Adam as representing differentiated form, we have an exact analogy of the sensory distraction that conditions the behaviour of susceptible man. It depicts the egoic complex, Adam; falling into reliance on defined data, that is eating the forbidden fruit; in response to personally experienced sensory modalities. Adam and Eve thus symbolise aspects of the power continuum, each contributing in a characteristic manner, to the progress towards egoic fixation. Since this is concerned with the rudimentary ontology of the fall, perhaps it could be called a new style of 'fundamentalism'.

But the Eden story illustrates much more than an outline of the egoic fixation processes. If we look more closely at its symbols, we can see depicted finer details of three stages operant in egoic fixation. We noted that to Eve the fruit appeared 'good for food', that she experienced it as 'pleasant', and then desired it to 'make wise'. That is, she illustrates a triad of inclination, associated pleasant experience, and resulting drive to grasp and appropriate.

This is exactly the sequence that we have already considered in the ontological analysis of the effects of pleasure clarification. The possibility is seen, that is, a preliminary vector occurs within the sentient continuum towards a particular form of its activity. The focus established is then known as pleasurable. As a result the focus and its pleasure are intensified and an apparent advantage acquired. We might describe this as a primal addiction. Thus the story depicts the changes operating as a particular form of action attracts such a degree of focus that its defined limits and associated functional possibilities are appropriated, while the constituent power is progressively ignored.

But as we noted earlier, it is not only a sense of pleasure that contributes to, and is changed by, such a process. The other modalities of the power continuum, including its sense of authority, are similarly changing. It may be difficult to investigate the sensations that are present and operant prior to and during the fixation process. But in meditation, or creative imagination exercises, it is possible to begin to glimpse at least a little of their nature. The sensation may await clearer insight, but this need not preclude us from considering its actuality. In

73

fact, as we shall discuss in more detail in a later chapter, such consideration can be a means of preparing for the awareness it indicates. Thus, although we may not find it easy to sense the nature of pre-egoic authority, we may usefully exercise our imagination in the way indicated by logical analysis towards a greater insight into the dynamism operant in the changes here being discussed. Like any in-break of personal awareness, the sensation to which we refer here will be more than an empirical logical assessment can define. But even so the exercise can help shed some light at this point.

So what can we now say of the pre-egoic authority? Since it is not limited or apparently divided by superstress on one form rather than another, it is the authority of the whole power continuum. This means that it is omnipotent, omniscient, and in the same moment, omnipresent. It is an authority that controls all, and from which nothing escapes. It is an all-pervading authority of the power continuum and, because it is not divided, it is immediate to every aspect of that power.

It is within such continuity of awareness that the processes occur that lead to the focus on separatist pursuit rather than all pervading authority. If we refer again to the Eden analogy, we can say that the garden depicts the continuum, the path pursued by Adam and Eve traces the orientation towards separativity, and their subsequent banishment represents the resulting self imposed fixation or limitation of awareness. Thus they are driven out of Eden, and an angel with a brandished sword illustrates the circumscribed operational zone to which they are now confined. This means that the sense of authority changes within the empirically orientated complex, the non-differentiated pre-egoic awareness now being usurped by the defined form set to pursue its divisive course.

With the progressive bias to the formally defined aspects of consciousness the sense of authority changes from that which is free to act as it will, to that confined to the particular zone. Instead of referring to an original creative intent not divorced from any aspect of the power continuum, the differentiated focus relies for its authority on its apparent particular capabilities. This is the fixation of the ego. The change could be likened to looking for water in a puddle rather than in an ocean. The structure that operates in such a separatist manner, forgetting the continuum in which it originates, believes the confined zone to be its 'self' and therefore acts to guard and increase its apparent capabilities. Hence it increasingly forgets the pre-egoic authority and assumes that it is its 'own' master.

A consequence of this transition is that empirically biased man often claims to have 'free will' and asserts that he can freely choose his course of action, even though a closer examination will show the deficiencies in such a statement. There is however, an element of truth in such a claim if it is taken to mean that the zone of power known as 'man' has itself elected to pursue the selective inclination and pleasure-pain bias leading into the fixation now established. In this sense it is ontologically correct to say that man does as he chooses. But it is not correct if he assumes it to mean that the separatist zone can now make a free, unbiased choice. It cannot; its choice is determined by the preference for pleasure repetition, pain avoidance and other inertic processes written into its substance.

Before we further intensify our review of egoic fixation, let us first summarise the three stages so far distinguished. We may describe them as prefer, posit and protect.

The preference is the first step; we may call it a fatal distraction. It is an orientation within the power continuum to incline in such a way towards one of its inherent possibilities that this acquires at that moment, relatively more stress than other modalities. It may be likened to a soloist stepping forward from a cosmic chorus. Such a vector is the first sign of preference and sets a path for the flow and probable bias of consciousness. A shift of awareness thus occurs so that a particular form receives greater emphasis while others are disregarded. The preference is therefore at once a preliminary expression of separatist pursuit and the means by which it can be strengthened. That is, it not only enacts the inclination, but reinforces it. And as a result there is an increasing movement towards separatist interest and pursuit. If we return to the analogy of the cosmic chorus, we could say that it is as if the emerging soloist progressively forgets the ranks from which he has come and which continue to lend him support.

Through biased pursuit of preference, consciousness can become so focused within a differentiated zone that its origin and actual continuing participation within the power continuum are forgotten. Instead it relies increasingly on skills it believes are posited for its 'own' use and can now be developed to his advantage. A being operating in this way, disregarding the power continuum, will naturally then fight to guard and increase its apparent acquisitions. Hence the three steps in the process of fixation are now evident, namely prefer, posit, and protect.

This triad is applicable to ordinary day to day experiences as well to a primal genesis of being. Which implies that here again the historical sequence is an image of dynamism operant in every moment of existence. We see expressions of these three steps in trivialities and matters of more importance. Perhaps it is an enticing cake that attracts our attention and becomes ours as we bite, digest and assimilate some of its ingredients. Or it may be a hoped for qualification, a goal that looms sufficiently strongly in our imagination to induce the required work so that in due course it becomes available for our use and protection. In these, and myriad other ways, the interest sets a course, the power is channelled accordingly, the effect incorporated, utilised and when needed, protected. The ordinary day to day processes of egoic attraction of interest, investment of effort, acquisition and due protection of effects thus reiterate the original course pursued as power moves towards an egoic bias.

There is therefore a continual recapitulation of the three steps involved in egoic fixation. And until this trend is recognised and revised it will continue to reinforce separatist ideas and pursuits. As long as egoic man is passive to this process he is liable to suffer the restriction of consciousness and associated inconvenience that it incurs. And the three steps of prefer, posit and protect will continue to dominate his actions.

One of the prime contributors to the unchecked repetition of this cycle is the belief that it is the only way to function, an attitude which is itself an effect of the process. As a result of inclination, separatist pleasure pursuit and protection of apparent assets, the continuum in which the now individuated zone arises is progressively forgotten. It is as if we recurrently and increasingly emphasise one note within a chord until it is so loud and clear that the other notes are drowned by its dominance. The progressive belief in separativity has an exactly similar effect within consciousness. Initially it is but one of many possibilities within the primal continuum, but with the stress, re-stress and eventually superstress it assumes dominance sufficient to mask other modes of awareness.

A similar sequence is seen in the dialectic of belief. On one hand, an active belief can afford a stability and strength which aids an investigation of life, while on the other hand, belief that has become inertic repetition can strangle and stultify in a manner that impedes a search for new insights and wider understanding. The attitude to ideology, or the way in which the consciousness operating in man relates to it, as well as its particular form, determines its effect. A passive belief assumed by a man for temporary convenience, with relatively little examination of why he adopts it and what it means to him in all the aspects of his being, is likely to inhibit his activities. But an active belief, constantly affirmed and consciously re-posited, becomes a vibrant, life enhancing experience. This principle is applicable to concepts related to any code.

In relation to the egoic complex this implies that there are two fundamentally opposed ways in which it can be operational. It is possible for man to be relatively passive to its formal aspect and rely in an inertic manner on the name defined assuming this to represent his 'self'. Or he can be working towards co-operation with the dynamic power continuum that constantly maintains such definition. His choice and pursuit of either of these courses will be strongly influenced by what he believes to be possible.

The contrasting possibilities of a form of action consciously affirmed within the power that constitutes it, or the exclusive reliance on the defined presentation while the causal dynamism is forgotten, can be illustrated very clearly in role-play techniques. In a dramatic presentation we see a role adopted by an actor for the purpose of the play. In that situation he knows it is a part taken up for a specific purpose and he is usually able to retract from its influence. But sometimes actors do not manage fully to disengage off-stage from their parts. We have heard an actor describe how whilst playing Shylock in 'The Merchant of Venice' his behaviour became so influenced by the role that at the end of the run he had to take the rest of the cast out for a drink in order to try to re-establish his more usual relationship with them. But this is unusual and actors are generally able to let go of their roles because they know they are temporary and not their only function.

The adoption of a role for a specific presentation can be traced back throughout history. Before the advent of staged drama, events were frequently recalled or celebrated in dance or in ritual. Here again roles were adopted for the purpose and duration of the event. There are many examples of this from diverse cultures. Role-play in dance and ritual has been, and still is, extensively used, for instance to invoke aid or celebrate success in relation to many activities. Examples relate to activities as diverse as planting and harvest, fertility, war or the affirmation of hierarchy. Such role-play spans the centuries, being part of every chapter of human development. But there is a danger that it could seem so familiar that we lose sight of its cardinal significance.

The instances of role-play, whether in dance, drama or ritual, illustrate not only the particular parts that are enacted, but also the phenomenon or process of role-play itself. We see a part performed and know that the performer has elected to comply with it. Perhaps it is because this is so obvious that we could overlook its deeper significance. The adoption of a role in dance or drama illustrates exactly the adoption of the egoic role by the true Self of man. In drama we know that the part is to be played for an evening, a week or perhaps a longer time. But off stage man appears to forget so readily that his egoic identification is similarly a role assumed for a time by his hidden and higher Self. Consequently he remains tied to the egoic demands. Just as a stage part is accepted for the purpose of a play, similarly the egoic part is assumed for a particular purpose in life. And if man forgets this he fixates on the egoic identification and assumes it to be his 'self' rather than affirming it as a role adopted by his higher Self for an evolutionary intent.

We can now see two main factors co-operating in the process of egoic fixation. On one side is the drive that is allowed to become fascinated by and preoccupied with the apparent success of the egoic complex. On the other side is the forgetfulness that is allowed to inhibit the awareness of the free, investigatory intent that first motivates the formative cycle within the power continuum. Thus through a combination of what it prefers to see, and what it elects to disregard, the egoic zone becomes increasingly preoccupied with its separatist pursuit. The inclination sets the path and inertia maintains it.

We have noted in a previous chapter that the term 'inertia' is used to refer to the continuation of a previously established mode of action. It therefore applies here to the drive to repeat pleasure and keep a blind eye turned towards a deeper awareness of being. Thus a role is rigidly maintained, with the result that man continues to believe that he is the part played. At the same time he largely forgets the causal aspect of his being that momentarily elects to play the role. Whatever the role accepted, be it mother, mechanic or mathematician, it is but a part and to forget this is to become tyrannised by its temporary application.

The belief that any man holds about himself exerts a major influence on the attitude he adopts and the experience he acquires. This is why we referred to it in the first chapter of this study, describing it as a 'governing concept'. If someone holds the belief that he/she is a 'gardener', a 'nurse' or a 'lecturer', and that this role is the limit of his/her person, then they are unlikely even to seek to understand the deeper aspects of the being electing to utilise such a commitment. When the belief that the role is the self exerts such dominance in consciousness, it is not over-stating the situation to describe it as 'tyrannised'. That is exactly what it is. The awareness that affirms the unique within the universal, the fixed within the free, is obscured by rigid, exclusive adherence to a particular code. And since the personal form of the belief and the attitude towards it can both be major contributors towards such obscuring, it is not irrelevant at this point to make an appropriate digression and take a closer look at the development and effects of ideology.

When we remember that man is a zone of power and that even the apparent solidity of his 'soma' is actually a force field, it is less difficult to consider the direct influence that belief can assert within being. Mental and physical forms are likewise manipulations of power; they are forces operating in specific ways. They are therefore able to interact with and modify the condensation of forces evidenced in a human being. Mechanical restraints can no longer be assumed to be the cardinal means of impeding man's activities. We now have scientific data and ontological insight to remind us that reason, as well as ropes, can restrain the experience and understanding of man.

It is the dialectic of belief, or reason, as we noted earlier, that it can enhance or inhibit awareness. Belief is not an optional extra that might make a difference to some beings. It is of fundamental importance and directly influences the experience of all men. It can be a standard affording a stability that enhances search and an expansion of consciousness. Or it can be a barrier that inhibits development as much as any iron bar. Just as the use of a name supports the structure and function of the developing ego complex, similarly the belief adopted acts within the experiential zone of the ego and modifies its subsequent activity. In the same way, the belief or idea concerning 'self' conditions a man's understanding and function. And the main stream of belief operating within a man is aptly described as his 'governing concept'.

Here again, the pleasure/pain vectors can play a major part. When we begin to explore the factors that determine the belief held by egoic man, a pleasure/pain bias is frequently found to contribute significantly to the process. Even with a merely superficial view it can be seen that the appeal of some forms of belief can be associated with a seeming temporary convenience. But in contrast, other ideologies can be off-putting to some people because they involve standards assessed as too difficult or demanding. An example of this type of conditioning occurred when an elderly lady from the East End of London appeared wearing a particular religious symbol that was new to her. When asked about it by her friends, she explained with a laugh, 'they do lovely suppers for us oldies'.

But with a closer analysis of the basis of belief, the effect of conditioning and pursuit of pleasure/pain vectors can be seen to operate in more subtle as well as relatively obvious ways. Psychotherapeutic practice has often shown examples of the less obvious types of conditioning that can influence personal belief. A specific one concerned a teenage girl with acute anxiety symptoms seemingly provoked after interaction with a particularly ardent religious sect. It emerged in therapy that the approach was reminiscent of a highly pressurised style of preaching experienced when she was a child during frequent visits to her grandmother. Although she had not appeared distressed during these experiences in her early years, the retained fear laden imprints were reactivated by the teenage encounter and overt anxiety was provoked. In therapy she discovered the particular similarities between the events and how the second encounter had provoked the previously contained memories. Through releasing and expressing at least some of the reactions involved, she was able to re-assess the roots of her symptoms. This work not only eased her anxiety symptoms, but also increased her insight into the way in which emotional imprints had biased her response to an assessment of particular ideas. After her work on the dynamics involved she found that she could make a clearer personal decision about which ideas she would choose to follow or reject.

Retained imprints of fear that man naturally prefers to avoid, or of pleasure that he would incline to repeat, can easily bias an assessment of ideas and result in their passive, unexamined rejection or acceptance. This principle applies whether the presented code concerns philosophy, politics, religion or any other system of thought. Unless we explore the roots of reactions to what we hear we are likely to remain passive to previously acquired pleasure/pain imprints and therefore vulnerable to their manipulation. An imprint of pleasurable effects incurred when following a particular dogma can incline a man automatically to adhere to that code. But latent reactions such as fear that he would usually prefer to avoid are likely passively to deter his interest. Not infrequently the pull of both vectors co-exist, in which case the stronger wins the day.

But let it be emphasised this is not suggesting that bias of this type is the only basis of man's belief. It may be a commonly seen factor, but it is not the only determinant involved. A 'free' choice of ideology implies that it is not determined by unresolved bias. Surely, an active belief is one that will stand up to this type of examination.

Pursuing this quest, if we take an even closer look at the determinants of belief, we will often find that the reaction to the manner of presentation is usually a relatively superficial factor. It is not only the attraction to an orator whose style may be reminiscent of an ancestral lover, or whose angry tones re-echo the shouts of a punitive patriarch that can determine man's response. The imprints go far deeper than this.

If in our creative imagination we go back to the primal dawn of man we may begin to sense that in the beginning, prior to the differentiation of distinct forms, there is an 'angst', or aura of anxiety associated with chaos and confusion. We may be able to sense an unease, a restless quivering that would be associated with a state of non-discrimination where possibilities are sensed but not defined to a known degree. It may be likened to the feeling of a child frightened of the dark, where a vivid imagination and an apparent lack of protection contribute to a highly alert, strained sense of fear. Shakespeare in Henry V describes such a situation. In the prologue to Act IV he recounts the scene prior to the battle of Agincourt:

> Now entertain conjecture of a time
> When creeping murmur and the poring dark
> Fills the wide vessel of the universe.
> From camp to camp through the foul womb of night
> The hum of either army stilly sounds,
> That the fix'd sentinels almost receive
> The secret whispers of each other's watch:
> Fire answers fire, and through their paly flames
> Each battle sees the other's umber'd face;
> Steed threatens steed, in high and boastful neighs
> Piercing the night's dull ear; and from the tents
> The armourers, accomplishing the knights,
> With busy hammers closing rivets up,
> Give dreadful note of preparation.

With the aid of such high poetry can we begin to imagine the unmitigated anxiety that precedes the clarification of action possibilities? And can we then go a step further and sense the contrast afforded when formal definition is established? If so we may realize, to at least some degree, the sense of strength, apparent security and pleasurable relief associated with achieving definition. And recalling that ideology, or established patterns of thought, as well as physical experience, contribute to egoic formation, we may sense that such apparent relief can apply to all aspects of a person.

In this way the 'pleasure in the edge' is experienced and the path set for its repetition. The sensory discrimination found within the initial creative act in due course contributes to the preference of egoic man for definitions concerning his 'self' and his 'environment'. And if taken a step further the accepted concepts, again in response to the pleasure bias, can become relatively fixated and exclusive. Thus an interaction of the fear of non-clarification and pleasure in achieving it, together contribute to a progressive identification with a particular code. And slowly but surely, the fixation of the ego is established.

But the relief of a primal anxiety is only one aspect of this process. Whilst on one hand it affords a deliverance from chaos, on the other it makes possible a new mode of fear, pain and inhibition of consciousness through opening up the possibility of separatist identification. In other words, once form is established, or a name defined, there is the extant danger of such stress being placed on it that the formative dynamism of the power continuum is forgotten. Hence with the clarification of form and relief of chaos there is immediately a risk of egoic fixation

Perhaps we are now beginning to approach the rudiments of primal conditioning. A progressive realization of such dynamics will involve the conscious affirmation of the particular experiential zone, the ego, as a channel or vehicle in and through which the dynamic continuum operates.

Until such awareness is attained, the pleasure experienced within the egoic complex will retain its attraction and draw the unwary towards repetitive, inertic identification. In this way the habitual identification and inertic pleasurable vectors, the progressive forgetfulness of the dynamic continuum, and the belief it can go its 'own' way, will all co-operate in the fixation of the ego.

In summary we may therefore say that the original authority is that of primal, intelligent power establishing within itself a form or structure of a functional order. The zone of such expressive form is willed by the Absolute as a locus of free response. But by virtue of its periphery it is subject to 'external' application of energy quanta and is therefore free to respond to these as it will. This fact, this possibility of choice, is the occasion of the fixation, or fall, of egoic awareness into identification with empirical data and separatist pleasure/pain pursuit.

Although the primal choice is essentially free in every moment, the establishment of the finite edge renders the form it freely posits vulnerable to reliance on finite data. It can therefore make errors and from its free choice introduce into itself a possibility of misinterpretation. It is precisely from this capacity that the empirical ego can focus on a system of defence to invasions from without and become fixated in its reliance on empirical processes.

But the authority of the encapsulated zone usurped in this manner is at once an occasion of fear as well as delight to its owner. The fixated focus, while applauding its apparent achievements, seeks to protect itself from invasion or loss. Which means that by its own action it incurs fear. The aggravation of such fear is one of the prime factors that in due course will contradict the pleasure attraction and contribute to the awakening of other modalities of awareness within the fixated ego, causing it to seek again the consciousness of the dynamic continuum.

Here we begin to consider the fulfilment of the ego.

Chapter 6: The Fulfilment of the Ego

In the previous chapter we discussed the way in which superstress on particular modalities of power leads to egoic limitation and ignorance of other aspects of the power continuum. The intent behind this chapter of our study is to discuss the reverse of such self inhibition. In this context the term 'fulfilment' is used to indicate a re-orientation of consciousness and rediscovery of its modalities previously veiled by empirical dominance. We will consider how this radical change will imply a growth of insight and enhancement of function affecting all aspects of being.

We have noted recurrently that the levels of human awareness cannot be divorced from one another, and that progressive personal insight corresponds with their enhanced interfunction. Thus to refer to egoic fulfilment does not imply an escape or release of being energies that might be assumed to leave the egoic vehicle and pass into realms previously divorced from them. That idea would imply an untenable dualism. In contrast, the fulfilment to be considered here affirms the on-going relevance and interaction of every aspect of being.

As understanding develops the significance of all the five levels of being previously discussed is seen in a new way. That is, the physical, emotive, intellectual, comprehensive and volitional processes become more valued and respected. It is a growing realization of the unique contribution made by each modality in fulfilling the function of the egoic vehicle and achieving Self understanding. This is the reverse of the empirical reliance that focuses onto a particular aspect of the self while neglecting wholeness, and may aptly be described as an increasing consciousness of consciousness. It is a change that affords finer awareness of the perception and performance of creative power and includes a deeper affirmation of egoic function. The fulfilment to which we refer here is therefore accompanied by increasing co-operation with the revelatory function originally vested within the egoic zone, and it is not an escapist ideology.

This means that the fulfilment we are now discussing is different from that sometimes assumed implied by this term. It is often suggested that ego fulfilment means 'getting your own way', or the satisfaction of empirical egotistic drive. But let it be emphasised this is not what is intended by the use of the term in our present context. The usual implication of 'getting your own way' is more accurately described as getting 'tied down'. We are referring to the reverse of this process in our present chapter and pursuing a wider yet deeper understanding of egoic function that is radically different from the appeasement of empirical ambition.

The words 'egoic fulfilment' are therefore applied here to refer to an in-break of awareness of the causal dynamism in and by which the ego is constituted. They imply the simultaneous comprehension, affirmation and transcendence of egoic limits. Or in other words, the fulfilment of egoic function is a momentary awareness of the causal, controlling aspect of the experienced phenomena, which although indicated by the act performed is not defined by it, and remains transcendent of it.

We can again use here the five-fold analysis of power, referring to the continual co-operation of impacted substantial energy, a flowing sentience, a discrete mentation, a comprehensive scan and the volition that controls all. The term fulfilment is used to imply a simultaneous awareness of these interfunctioning modalities, while 'egoic fulfilment' indicates the conscious operation of the egoic complex in their manifestation.

Such a fulfilment is necessarily an awareness that transcends the ordinary empirical egoic aim. If we are to understand and control the ego, which its 'fulfilment' implies, we have to find again the awareness of the causal aspect of power that conceives and controls its course. Although this means that the evolving ego is not 'getting its own way' in the sense of achieving ordinarily defined objectives, to a deeper awareness its 'own way' is being attained. If we overcome the habitual reliance on empirical definition and remember that the true causal intent is a higher aspect of the power operating in a specified manner, we can correctly say that an egoic zone is getting its own way. It depends on where we focus, or how we look at the situation. Where we are over-identified with the form posited we are likely to feel that discovering an awareness that directs and maintains it could constitute a threat to private purpose. But the reaction is different if we begin to focus more on the causal intent that is not alien to the form. The point of view adopted determines the assessment of the situation.

So here at the beginning of this chapter let us emphasise that egoic fulfilment does not imply an achievement of the aims and objectives set by an egoic complex assuming that its empirical data are its totality. Instead the fulfilment referred to is the growth of consciousness towards a greater awareness of the modalities of power that define and operate through that complex. We have stressed this point in the hope that it will avert some of the confusion that is so often associated with concepts relating to ego fulfilment.

Such a change is a momentary experience, or to use the term employed by Kierkegaard, it is of the 'instant'. Fulfilment implies an awareness of all five aspects of the power operating in and through the ego; less than this would not be a true fulfilment of awareness. Therefore it indicates a consciousness of the immediate intention in every moment. It is a 'now' awareness, cognisant of the intent to act in the moment of its action. That is, fulfilment truly realized cannot be other than immediate, or of the instant. Any lesser insight would be inertic adherence to previously established modes of action with varying degrees of forgetfulness of the initiating will.

But here again we can observe a linear developmental cycle that depicts processes that are essentially immediate. In relation to the involution of power to generate particular modes of action, we observed that the serial presentation of graduated phases reflects the processes of a creative dynamism operating in every moment of existence. A similar principle applies concerning egoic fulfilment where the re-orientation that is an immediate act of will is also illustrated by a gradual development of insight. It is therefore possible, through the observation of changes that occur as understanding unfolds, to reflect on an in-break of awareness that fully realized cannot be other than immediate.

Any subject presented to man rarely receives much attention until his interest in it is sufficiently aroused. Egoic fulfilment is no exception to this principle. One of the first lines of consideration relevant to the re-orientation of awareness is therefore concerned with the factors that provoke an interest in the possibility of it happening.

Here we can observe negative and positive aspects of the process. As we continue this section of our study we will discuss the way in which these function as two vectoral streams which may at first appear contradictory, but on closer analysis are seen to be complementary in their contribution towards egoic fulfilment.

At the end of the previous chapter we made a preliminary reference to the way in which an increase of fear can play a part in revealing the inadequacy of being tied to ordinary empirically defined limits. We could call this the negative vector or aspect of the process we are now considering. The accompanying positive vector, that may even dominate such fear, is a growing interest in developmental possibilities and a related search for greater understanding. That is, on one hand there can be fear of deficiency, and on the other an interest in greater sufficiency. Since these two vectors often serve as prime movers in the progression towards egoic fulfilment we will look at each of them in more detail.

We have referred to the sensory change that can occur when the egoic complex apparently achieves a stable form, namely that the awareness of identity, authority and prowess can all be experienced in a new and attractive manner. But such definition is obviously ambiguous since the referential edge that includes and affords pleasurable success, also excludes and becomes a cause of threat. We will consider how in due course, this dual effect supports a growing interest in overcoming restrictive egoic pursuits.

It is relevant here to revisit a principle considered in the previous chapter concerning the contrasts between the effects of pleasure and pain in reinforcing or challenging egoic limits. We noted that pleasure is an awareness associated with assimilable stimuli and pain incurred when the input cannot be readily integrated in this way. This led onto the observation that pain effects, and associated sub-cortical data, can be re-assessed after receipt and aligned in a manner that not only decreases pain but also increases personal insight.

But it is obvious that ordinary man is less likely to desire to rectify a pleasant sensation which is therefore liable to be retained as a relatively enduring impression within his being. We may also deduce here that a greater assimilation capacity will heighten the awareness of pleasure and so could, if it was allowed to do so, increase the trap for egoic reliance on its effects. But such pleasure discrimination will co-incidentally incur fear of its loss. That is, fear can redress the balance and rectify what could otherwise easily become an undisputed bias within consciousness. The ambiguity of pleasure, that is the fear of loss that accompanies it, is the equilibration without which repetitive pleasure stimuli could constitute an unguarded trap.

Many philosophers and other writers have referred to this dialectical principle. To quote but one example, in the writings of Taoism attributed to Lao Tzu we read:

> Since the world points up beauty as such,
> There is ugliness too.
> If goodness is taken as goodness,
> Wickedness enters as well.
>
> For is and is-not come together,
> Hard and easy are complementary,
> Long and short are relative,
> High and low are comparative.[1]

Just as ugliness is the corollary of beauty, and good of evil, similarly pain and fear contrast pleasure and success. They therefore afford a balance which averts the possibility of an unopposed bias within consciousness.

So what does this imply in relation to egoic function and fulfilment? Namely that energy inputs received and interpreted as pleasurable contain within them the seeds of fear that will eventually provoke sufficient disquiet to prevent total submission to repetitive action. The fear of failure, loss, pain or other experiences defined as unpleasant or unwanted, are aspects of awareness that prevent total complacency. That is, fear is like a sentinel within the psyche provoking sufficient alertness to prevent a degree of complacency that could be tantamount to death.

---

[1] 'The Way of Life', Lao Tzu. Poem 2, page 54. Trans. R. B. Blakney, Pub. Mentor, 1955

Life implies an awareness of what is happening and an ability to change in relation to it. If the egoic complex became so trapped that it saw no need to do other than repeat a particular mode of action to obtain a known response, it would be dead to other possibilities. The fear, that is the partner of pleasure, is therefore the force that plays a major part in the prevention of such servitude. And whilst an egoic being finds experience that it would like to repeat, the fear that such repetition might be difficult, and the awareness that there could be another means of even greater satisfaction, together prevent a complete reliance on one particular form of action. Here is yet another example of the principle that opposition is a basis for insight. Through the contrasting effects of achievement and pleasure on one side, with fear and pain on the other, not only are both known more clearly, but also the incentive to seek new modes of experience is heightened.

Here we are noting what we may term the paradox of fear. Whilst it is obviously unpleasant and may restrict activity, it can also contribute to human development by reducing a bias of consciousness.

We may also note another aspect to this cycle. A state of fear usually implies an awareness of an unknown, or sensing a threat that is not adequately comprehended or controlled by the one who fears. Or it may be that the feared object or state, though known and understood to some degree, is believed to assert a measure of power that cannot be countered by the being who experiences the fear. For example, a child may show a dread of darkness, cringing from what it might contain. Or it might fear a dog, which though controlled, recognised and named appropriately, constitutes a threat because of its size and power, both of which may provoke prior conditioning in the child. In both of these situations fear is experienced because the child's identity is with an organism unable to control the reactions evoked. This may be described as stating the obvious, but it has implications that are highly relevant to our study of egoic fulfilment.

The fear experienced in similar encounters is not only due to the discrepancies in size, strength or other capabilities of the organisms involved. In addition to such obvious factors there are others that are more subtle but no less important. Fear is nurtured when the consciousness is exclusively identified with the empirical data that concern it. This type of exclusive identification is associated with personally biased attainments and objectives, and when these appear threatened, empirical egoic man is likely to interpret the challenge as a threat to his 'self'. That is, the repetitive stress associated with the fixation of an exclusively identified ego itself incurs fear of disruption and even of destruction. Over identification with empirical aspects of being, with exclusive reliance on past attainments, plays a major part in the aggravation of fear. Hence we increasingly realize the ambiguity of the 'pleasure in the edge' or the definition of a personal zone of activity. Namely that while it rescues from uncertainty in a way that affords clarity, it is also able to nurture egoic fear and frustration.

A further outcome of this cycle concerns reactions between egoic beings. Where man is governed by concepts of empirical identification he is naturally inclined to protect his apparent attainments and preferably increase them. But at the same time he will apply a similar concept in relation to his colleagues and assume that they are likewise seeking to acquire whatever they believe they need to enhance their own prowess. Which means that an empirically biased man, by his own action, can nurture progressive reasons for suspecting that other beings might acquire greater powers, or even usurp resources which he regards as vital to his own needs. Such concepts can then intensify egoic fear and envy

Examples of this are an everyday occurrence. But consideration of its ontological basis affords an insight into the development of fear and the increase of extant opposition between men as evolution proceeds. It is like a game of marbles, the faster one rolls, the harder it strikes and propels others encountered along its path. Or in other words, egotism provokes egotism. But even this cycle can contribute to evolution when, in due course, the fear and frustration incurred through empirical egoic dominance contribute to the provocation of interest in other modes of egoic fulfilment.

But it is not only such relatively outward looking processes which thus contribute to the negative vectors instrumental in the change of an egoic orientation. Co-operating with these are other psychological vectors provoked within man. Amongst these, two that are particularly prominent are first, the conflict described as occurring between the id, ego, and superego; and second, the frustration associated with finding that knowledge always seems to alert a need to know more.

When we considered the 'The Further Development of the Ego' in Chapter 3 of this study, we referred to the interaction between the aspects of the psyche termed by Freud the 'id', 'ego' and 'superego'. This assessment is again relevant in our continuing study. The 'id', the impulsive drive, provokes an action, which is experienced as far as reality permits by the 'ego', while the domineering 'superego', or law setter, takes note and restrains or allows activity to continue according to whether or not it accords with previously formulated taboos or ideals. This cycle can be a useful source of endless conflict within man when it becomes one of the vectors provoking a search for new ways of understanding and operating through the egoic complex.

The second major provocation of personal inner frustration is associated with a dawning awareness of the deficiency of knowledge. An empirically identified man frequently finds that even a detailed study of a specific subject reveals a need to learn yet more about it. That is, the more he learns, the more he finds there is to learn. Anatomy and physiology are particularly clear examples of this. A study of the structure and function of organs leads onto a study of the cells they contain, then of the components of the cells, and then to further studies of the yet finer details, with all these stages affording self-perpetuating cycles. Whilst this can be exciting, to empirically identified man it can also be frustrating since it awakens an awareness that knowledge continually provokes an awareness of its own limits and the need for more knowledge.

This means that if individual knowledge and success are the dominant aims of an ego-identified person, then that person is likely to become increasingly depressed. It is a negative phase of egoic frustration that can be a basic factor in the aetiology of depressive illness.

But this is not, of course, the only way of experiencing the egoic function. Even such a negative stage can in due course serve an evolutionary purpose useful to the person experiencing it and to other people learning with him. Empirical reliance, having been thoroughly tried and tested from enough angles to convince a being of its deficiency, can provoke a change of interest. This change, a re-orientation, can be a readiness to seek new modes of egoic function, new possibilities of action. Hence the frustration and fear incurred by empirical dominance may contribute to a re-orientation such that man begins to look beyond the ordinary bounds for egoic fulfilment.

So far we have considered negative vectors that can influence the re-orientation of an egoic man. But what can we say of the positive factors similarly involved, and perhaps acting as a dominant influence? Here the emphasis shifts and a new mode of awareness is sought, not so much because inadequacy impels it, but because the awareness sensed possible itself draws the interest.

Although a man predominantly identified with personally proven data largely forgets other aspects of the power continuum, they are present and operant within him. Forgetfulness may apparently restrain a wider and deeper awareness, but it does not annihilate it. Sometimes a sense that goes beyond the empirical limits breaks through as the so-called 'sixth sense', or 'intuition', serving as a reminder to man that modes of consciousness, not bound by ordinarily defined data, are within his field of experience. It is as if a rudimentary awareness begins to re-assert itself within the consciousness operating within man.

This change is easier to understand if we recall that egoic man exists within a dynamic continuum from which he is never separated. The re-orientation can then be envisaged as a re-assertion of a modality of power innate to his being, and not an influx or visitation of a force deemed higher and somehow previously separate from him in the manner suggested by some dualistic interpretations of religious concepts. The awareness is continually within man, it may be masked by forgetfulness but is not removed from or made alien to him. Here again the five-fold analysis of power operating in every moment within man is relevant. The modalities of consciousness that we may describe as 'finer' or 'higher' than those ordinarily experienced are always present, though commonly disregarded.

Today the two vectoral streams that contribute to a re-orientation of interest in all aspects of egoic activity are widely experienced. The progressive disillusionment and fear that constitute the negative flux may at first appear to suppress a growing interest in more subtle aspects of life experience. But on closer analysis these two seemingly contrasting factors can be seen to co-operate when together they provoke the re-orientation of consciousness vital to the further development of egoic man. Their combined effects can be very important in the ongoing evolution of human consciousness.

In many human experiences due consideration of the factors involved is a precursor to the actual performance. The re-orientation of egoic awareness is no exception to this principle and due reflection on the processes involved can prove to be part of the preparation for the actual realization. Our next stage in this study is therefore to intensify our consideration of the processes involved and how they can be increasingly applied in action.

We may describe the converging effects of the positive and negative factors provoking re-orientation as a conspiracy of old and new ways. That is, a re-orientation of egoic consciousness is provoked by the combined effects of progressive frustration incurred by old habits relating to separatist goals, and the awakening excitement that accompanies new insight relating to true Self direction and inter-function.

We have seen that action based on exclusive empiricism and ignorance of the immediate dynamism of being is bound to fail. It is not only that man wants the greener grass on the other side of the fence. The consciousness hidden within his being, the awareness that he is a function within a sentient continuum, will never be content with or restrained by such inertic empiricism. That is, it is not only the want for more goods, richer relationships or more powerful principles, which provoke dissatisfaction in sentient beings. It is an inner awareness, veiled but not annihilated, that will never be content with less than a return to immediate affirmation of the dynamic continuum.

A paradox of empirical egoic pursuit is that in due course it contributes to its own reversal. The progressive inner restless dissatisfaction provoked by the empirically biased activity, gradually alerts the individual functioning in this manner and enhances a personal readiness for a new mode of egoic fulfilment. Since 'love' implies the will to seek the highest possible development, the incentive to which we here refer is the Self love which will not be appeased by any less than immediate consciousness of its own dynamic intentionality. It seeks the highest for itself, and that implies an awareness of its origin and control in the Absolute non-dual continuum.

As such awareness beckons we may begin to experience anew the co-operation between the vectoral streams relevant to egoic re-orientation and fulfilment. On one hand the rebuff incurred by empirical dominance, and on the other the hidden though innate awareness of the continuum, co-operate in leading man to seek new modes of action. These contrasting vectors work together inducing a gradual re-direction and application of a personal egoic commitment.

But at the same time, there is also a continuing natural opposition to the process. Recurrently, previously established inertia will attempt to pull the individual focus back towards repetitive reliance on apparent attainments whether they are substantial goods, relationships or ideologies. The inertic pressure of empirical pursuit is such that if man allows any glimmer of hope that attainment of a privately selected goal can fully meet his sense of need, he is likely to go on targeting his particular objective. Hence a long and thorough investigation of empirical reliance and rebuff is often required before the inertic bias is radically changed. And until such a re-orientation occurs, egoic man not only remains personally dominated by his previously established preferences, but also commonly pours scorn on ideas relating to the possibility of changing course.

This inertic cycle might at first appear only to maintain the pursuit of a particular goal. But as we have already noted, the cycle is paradoxical since it is also nurturing changes that in due course contribute to the disruption of its bias. With the intensification of interest in the objective, and heightened reactivity if thwarted, a point is gradually approached where the energies provoked are more than can be assimilated by the system previously defined. The frictive effect of unassimilated energy may then result in a flash of insight and change of attitude towards the erstwhile objective. That is, the available energy becomes more than can be applied in the manner previously pursued and supports a search for new modes of operation.

But here again, the breakdown of a restrictive bias is only one side of the process. If there was no concomitant realignment, inertia could revert to chaos. Here we return to the principle of the contrasting though co-operative vectors contributing to egoic re-orientation. On one hand the progressive frustration mobilises and releases reserves of psychological energies. While on the other hand, man's innate awareness draws him to formulate clearer concepts concerning life's experiences and aspirations. Such concepts then offer new pathways for the released energies to follow.

We have previously discussed similar principles in relation to the effects of ideology. It is as if it the newly defined concepts afford a plan according to which various psychological energies can be channelled and afford scope for further assessment. Which means that progressively clarifying concepts concerning the processes operating within all aspects of our person is of fundamental importance in the movement towards egoic fulfilment.

Although we have stressed the transitional nature of ideology we are in no way minimising its value. It acts as a measure in relation to which psychological energies can be progressively investigated and revealed. Lord Balfour expressed the need for on-going clarification of concepts very clearly in a poem. He wrote:

Our highest truths are but half truths,
Think not to settle down for ever in any truth.
Make use of it as a tent in which to pass a Summer's night,
But build no house of it, or it will be a tomb.
When you first have an inkling of its insufficiency
And begin to descry a dim counter truth looming up beyond,
Then weep not, but give thanks:
It is the Lord's voice whispering
'Take up thy bed and walk'.[2]

This poem reminds us that while we seek to clarify concepts to channel the newly released psychological energies, at the same time we need to maintain a constant readiness to readjust them. The contrasting vectoral streams that we are considering co-operate in this process.

---

[2] Arthur James Balfour, 1848-1930

Whilst the frictive energy requires channels to direct it, the inner awareness will not be appeased by a mere repetition of inertic courses. Both aspects require an active, or immediate, clarification of concepts relevant to the awareness being disclosed.

And so, aided by the continuing co-operation of these vectors, what may we now say of the factors that determine the revelation of consciousness that we are here describing as egoic fulfilment? Can we say other than that primarily it is an act of will? The five-fold analysis of power would support this insight. To temporal man it can only be construed as 'grace', that is, the disclosure of an awareness previously forgotten and beyond his empirical control. But the many references of mystic writers to a consciousness of non-duality between the self and creative power, imply that in the moment of deeper insight the awareness that we are here referring to as 'will' is recognised to be not-other-than the Self. The realization of such awareness may be glimpsed, or may yet await us. But even so, the consideration of logical principles relevant to it can be a means of preparing for further disclosure.

We have previously described the will as unseen but reflected by other aspects of the power continuum. If we apply this principle here, we can say that the will to rediscover aspects of consciousness previously forgotten by man can be applied in relation to each of the modalities of power operating within him. That is, all the levels of his awareness may be investigated and applied in a manner that co-operates with an intent to rediscover new modes of personal awareness in the pursuit of egoic fulfilment.

Starting at the basic physical level of experience we can investigate and apply a diet, exercise and rest regime that is appropriate for personal health. Most people are well aware that due care over such basic requirements will assist healthy function whereas neglect will progressively impede it. So if we are determined to pursue the search for increased personal awareness we start at the physical level by finding a regime suited to our individual needs and use it intelligently.

When we reflect on emotional processes we can progressively observe their nature and effects, increase our understanding of how they are provoked and at times modify their impact.

At the level of mentation we can consider ideas relevant to our individual life experience. We can formulate concepts as we seek to asses physical and emotional aspects of our personal actions. These concepts can be further clarified as we compare our experiences and assessments of them, with the ideas shared by other people. Reading and study, especially of ideas shared by the world's great thinkers, offer further major resources. Reflection on concepts shared throughout human history can be a very helpful challenge and radically assist the search for aspects of awareness that might otherwise remain forgotten.

In the further application of deeper insight valuable help has often been assisted by a careful use of ritual, prayer, meditation or similar activities. The practices helpful to an individual may be those of religious or philosophic foundations, or any other group of people seeking to understand the nature of being and its co-operation with the causal aspects of power. In such practices the physical movements and sound expressions can reinforce the discernment and substantialisation of insight into the co-operant aspects of consciousness. The physical movement, the sensory awareness, the formulation of sound, the understanding of the interfunction of these three aspects, and progressive reflection on the intent to apply to the exercise, all co-operate in the self revelation of power.

Such a search will always be an individual quest. Even when insights are usefully shared with other people intent on similar investigations, the path will remain essentially unique to the searcher. Finding and using an individually helpful regime for physical well-being, clarifying insightful concepts and appropriately using ritual or similar activities focused on increasing Self awareness, can all assist an individual seeking the re-orientation here described as egoic fulfilment.

Such aids to re-orientation are but some of the formal modes of activity pursued throughout human history to assist man in the quest to become more aware of the power operating within him. Many writings of mystics and other researchers have testified to the role of such practices in a search for insight.

Here we may experience a progressive cycle of insight as man becomes more alert, more aware of the dynamic nature of being. As the increasing insight aids further application to training practices, their use is enhanced, further insight is supported, and so on. In this cyclic development a true Self consciousness becomes an ongoing revelation, the innate awareness in man continually drawing him to look for finer insight and to use more effectively the steps that assist its ongoing disclosure.

Through the continuing co-operation of the two vectoral streams, namely empirical frustration and innate awareness leading man to look for new modes of fulfilment, the being energies are gradually redirected and a point approached at which re-orientation occurs. This may be described as an 'inversion' of awareness, since instead of turning outwards to empirically defined constructs, the interest inverts towards an increased co-operation with the causal aspect, the will of being.

As we noted in the preliminary stages of this part of our study, this change is immediate to the moment and not merely a 'once-in-a-lifetime' occurrence. The application of interest here considered is momentary, a 'now' orientation. Here again, the linear presentation of the process is an image of an immediate application of consciousness. Of course there may be moments in a man's life when he is particularly aware that his interests are changing. But the linear events reflect a dynamism that is also non-linear. Interest is not vectored at one time and set to run for X hours, days or years. It is always of the moment.

In the course of time we may see a serial sequence as one personally biased pursuit after another is tried, tested and given up. But this is again an image of what, in due course, will become a non-serial process. It illustrates the supreme moment of non-identification of creativity: an awareness which, though it is conscious of the forms it creates, refuses to identify with them and therefore remains free to act as it will. It is as if it senses the limitation, fear and frustration that would be incurred by over-identification and refuses to be drawn into it. In this moment there is an immediate as well as linear appreciation of potential restriction and an abandonment which releases from its hold. But such a process implies a full understanding of its effects. We could say that empiricism is only given up when it has been thoroughly investigated, or at least investigated sufficiently to convince the being energies of its outcome.

This is the essence of prodigality, that is, of going the whole hog before undergoing the metanoia that constitutes repentance. Such a change is the inversion to which we have referred. It is an immediate act of will. It is momentary, and not merely linear.

We noted at the beginning of this chapter that the fulfilment to which we are referring does not mean the ordinary type of 'getting your own way'. The more we pursue these studies, the clearer this fact becomes.

At the same time it is also increasingly apparent that the fulfilment envisaged is not merely a renunciation or denial. It is, as the term fulfilment implies, an attainment. It refers to a re-orientation that enables the egoic 'unit' with its concrete, empirical experience, to be seen and accepted in an entirely new way. That is, an awareness develops of the egoic complex in relation to the aspects of power which, though previously forgotten, are not divorced from it and constitute its formal manifestations. These erstwhile ignored modalities of consciousness may be described as the 'true' or 'higher' Self and the insight into their operation at once embraces and exceeds the limits of defined data.

At this point empirical thinkers may be inclined to groan and say we are stepping beyond proven facts into realms of 'fanciful speculation'. But this need not be so. Although we are beginning to consider levels of awareness that lie beyond the ordinary definitions and data, we can continue to apply logical principles in our approach. The consciousness we explore may transcend the restraint of reason, but even so logic and reason can be used as we reflect on it.

The concepts formulated, and the egoic complex through which they are expressed, are constructs within the power continuum. It therefore follows that if we are to approach an adequacy of understanding of these or any other constructs, we cannot ignore any of the modalities of power in and by which they are constituted. That is, if we are to find more understanding of the ego, and work towards its fulfilment, we need to reflect not only on the linear life style of forces assimilated to it, but on the creative intent intrinsic to it. But intentionality, or an application of will, is immediate to the moment of operation. Therefore, although the form posited indicates its operation, it cannot define it. Like the lightening flash that shoots across the sky, its speed is too great for ordinary analysis. Nothing less than immediate recognition can be the basis of true realization of will. Logical principles that support such insight are therefore at once affirmed and transcended.

So what may we now say of the fulfilment of the ego? We can observe that the two vectoral streams, progressive empirical rebuff, and an emergence of the innate awareness of other modalities of power, contribute to a new stage in the development of egoic man. Here he admits to a sense of need, but he no longer expects an outward, inertically defined target to afford an adequate answer. At this point re-orientation is possible. It is made substantial when the consciousness operating in man, ceasing to look for an answer in a form or change of situation dependent on events 'outside' himself, accepts and co-operates with the awareness that fulfilment lies primarily in a disclosure of the constituent dynamism of all things.

We have previously noted that an increase of insight may be approached by a logical analysis. Such an investigation, concurrent with the re-assertion of the deeper awareness innate to man, can strongly support a rediscovery of intentionality. The growth of insight may also be enhanced by a thorough repudiation of empirical reliance on the myriad objectives available to egoic man. A negative outcome of the progressive realization of the inadequacy of empirically biased objectives could be apathy and depression. But in its positive phase, where a being learns actively to wait in readiness for a change sensed to be possible though as yet unknown, it is highly alert. Such waiting is not the discontented apathy that drifts with any whim that next appeals to its fancy. Instead it is a highly refined discrimination, alert to avoid falling back into a repetition of empirical reliance.

In Buddhist philosophy such a developmental stage is illustrated in the temptations of the Buddha by Mara. Despite using various guises planned to distract the Buddha and avert his search for enlightenment, Mara fails and the Buddha completes his quest. His steady insistence on saying 'no' to all distractions enables the Buddha to find the inner illumination he seeks.

In ontological terms we may refer to this process as a deliberate intensification of awareness. Its negative aspect is the absolute refusal of a being to peripheralise, that is, to let a form posited by and within consciousness acquire such stress that it temporarily over rules its central awareness of the creative process. In other words, it is a refusal to follow the inclination that could easily incur forgetfulness of the dynamic intent and fall back to reliance on an extant form, whether this is associated with position, relationship or any other objective.

But let it be quickly added at this point that these insights do not imply a need for abstinence or withdrawal from contracts or other commitments associated with social activities, business, relationships or other similar experiences. We are referring here to a change of attitude towards such contacts rather than abstention from them. It means they will be approached in a new way not tied to empirical conquest. When relationships are not relied on to meet egoic need, they are more likely to become a useful means of reflexion and enhance the development of greater personal insight into the nature of encounter. A relationship of any sort can be improved if it is based on choice rather than need. Whatever the extant situation, the change to which we refer here when we talk of the deliberate intensification of consciousness and an associated refusal to peripheralise, involves the withdrawal from reliance on that extant environment.

The positive phase of such a re-orientation is experienced as inner readiness to wait for a change of awareness to which logical analysis points and of which glimmers at times begin to occur. It is a sensation with new levels of interest and quiet satisfaction; a quality of awareness denied by empirical reliance just as the piping sounds of a piccolo may be masked by clamorous brass. Such insight begins to occur in the moment in which the refusal to peripheralise and rely on ordinary, empirical phenomena, co-operates with an intense in-holding of awareness in readiness for new modes of consciousness. At this point we begin to realize more of what is implied by the words 'the metanoia that constitutes repentance'.

Gradually the point may be approached where, although egoic man admits to a state of need, he also realizes that from an empirical basis he cannot determine a course that will satisfy his needs. At this

102

stage in development the hidden awareness in man of his origin within the power continuum, together with concepts beginning to be formulated in relation to this awareness, may be realized in a new way. The theological term that may be used to describe this is 'waiting on grace'. It implies a conscious affirmation within man that ordinary, empirically proven data are neither enough to appease his deeper sense of need, or to indicate other objectives that might afford satisfaction. A change then occurs within his consciousness such that instead of turning back to reliance on an externalised, formal construct, be it personal, ideological or material, there is a deliberate intensification of awareness. It is the metanoia of repentance that reverses the erstwhile outward dependence on form and is accompanied in the same moment by an inversion that is the conscious affirmation of the dynamism that makes form possible.

Such an in-holding of awareness therefore intensifies and transforms the consciousness of being. If the outlet for any force is denied, be it water, air or heat, it will build up until either it bursts out from the impeding vessel or changes its own state. A similar change can occur within the being of man. Through the intensification of his consciousness a point may be reached where his awareness begins to change radically and approach a quality that may be referred to as a 'fulfilment'.

In this moment the egoic channel is transformed to become a vehicle for the Self-reflexion of consciousness. There is at once a new awareness of the sensation and concepts relating to the not-twoness of modalities of power within a continuum. There is recognition of the consciousness to which phrases like 'the interfunction of all forms within a field of power' seek to refer. Here the being does not need to find something 'outside' to appease, it begins to feel a sufficiency in the co-operant modalities of dynamism internal to the Self. Here it begins to realize an awareness that can be said to 'have need of nothing', yet be able to enjoy 'all things added'.

In this moment it appreciates anew that deliberate intensification of consciousness is the key to fulfilment. It begins to recognise an awareness implied by words such as 'creative intentionality'. It begins to be aware of the intent that maintains its being and feels a precision of control compared to which empirical antics are ineffective. In abandoning to grace it finds a security vastly superior to anything it has previously conceived possible.

In the writings of Jacob Boehme this process is likened to the heating of an iron poker to the point where it will incandesce. The heat of the iron increases until it is such that the iron is apparently raised from its dull condition as a nearly inert metal, to a glowing, more vibrant form of power. The change is analogous to that occurring within the psyche of man when the intensification of forces operant within it approaches a point at which they are no longer containable in the manner previously known. Consciousness may then arc back to the awareness of its origin. Boehme calls this the 'feuerschrack', the shriek of the fire. Along with several other philosophers, Boehme likens the source of creation to fire. Hence he uses the term 'feuerschrack' to depict the return to the awareness of the primal creative aspect of power. We speak of it as a 'return' because that is precisely how it is experienced. The change to which it refers is a rediscovery of an awareness that in the moment of realization is known to have been eternally present. 'Feuerschrack' is a momentary occurrence, an immediate release from empirical dominance and a return to awareness of the dynamism that makes egoic experience possible.

We may now ask what more can be said of the consciousness to which such re-orientation leads? It is a level of insight that embraces and defines form whilst it also transcends it. Form is necessarily limited. But the initiative that emits form, whilst it affirms the boundary it posits, is more than the construct can describe. Time and form are measurable entities, determined according to established limits. But the initiative that propagates them is instantaneous in its awareness and operation and therefore beyond the restraint of the linear time forms it posits. The immediacy of the creative intent is too quick for temporal analysis and, precisely because of this, is associated with a comprehensive view of experience.

A glimpse of this possibility can occur when we experience a 'flash of inspiration'. Sometimes thorough study of data new to us can lead to a sudden in-break of awareness that enables us momentarily to fit them together and understand at least some of their implications. It can be a moment of illumination suddenly opening up our understanding of ideas and their relevance for us.

It is sometimes assumed that a similar change of egoic awareness would be an end point, or some sort of conclusion to an evolutionary process. But whether we begin to glimpse the sensation of re-orientation, or evaluate it as a logical possibility, we can see that rather than being an end or termination of an evolutionary process, it is a beginning of a new mode of action. It is an in-break of awareness that puts the ego in its rightful place as a vehicle for the Self-reflexion of consciousness and therefore enables its true function to begin.

If we understand more about the workings of the tools we use we are more likely to employ them to their optimum. Similarly with the egoic complex, as we approach a greater insight into the power that maintains it and the function for which it is fitted, the instrument is better utilised and understanding further developed. That is, a finer comprehension and performance of the egoic function leads to an increased awareness of the power that constitutes it, and in turn the growing insight leads to enhanced functional activity. Thus the enlightenment is ongoing and the reverse of the vicious circle associated with egoic fixation.

Within any being there is an innate awareness of its optimal function. All power is sentient and knows within itself the performance of which it is capable. Hence the persistent unease of a man who knows he is not operating at his optimal level. The power that constitutes man is aware of the reflexive, revelatory function invested within him. This means that the egoic complex, unable to rest under the constraint of a non-reflexive empirical bias, drives on towards a greater fulfilment of its potential. And when man discerns an awareness that fulfils, he knows this is not an end to development, but a change better described as a new beginning of greater function.

Confusion has sometimes arisen in relation to these ideas when philosophies of Hinduism and Buddhism are interpreted as searching for an 'escape from reality' into an undifferentiated 'bliss' of Brahman or Nirvana. Ideas of 'transcendence' are commonly assumed to have similar escapist implications. But this is not an interpretation accepted in this study.

The Christian ethics and incarnation illustrate that transcendence is found by affirming the bodily commitment to an extreme degree. That is, that fulfilment is attained in and through a thorough application to physical experience rather than by some sort of escape from its operations.

A true enactment of egoic function, since it involves insight into all five levels of awareness previously discussed in this study, is an immediate, unique, momentary occurrence and revelation. We can say further that the five-fold interfunction is an eternal recurrence, a cycle re-iterated in every existential moment. It is this recurrence that maintains the created order in both its immediate and linear aspects. Hence it is not merely that at some far distant moment in primal history a 'big bang' occurred and set in motion a series of changes. The creative intent is immediately operant in every moment of time. Just as time presupposes the trans-temporal, form implies the trans-form. Wherever there is time or form there is now an awareness that both transcends and accepts such restraint. It is as operant now as at any primal moment in the dawn of the world, or of the egoic reference, that we say we 'know'.

Since we are beginning to consider the aspect of creative power, which transcends time, namely the parachronic, the use of finitely negative expressions is inevitable. It is dialectical that an extreme affirmation is the pathway to a level of consciousness transcendent of time, form and words, and for which only negative expressions and silence are therefore appropriate.

Hence Buddhism and Western mysticism refer to the way of the 'great negation'. While Christian doctrines and the Easter events emphasise even more strongly that the release of awareness and negation of temporal limitations is found through the degree of commitment to time and place affirmed in the paradox of the crucifixion. The dialectical principle of transcendence of time or form through affirmation of these experiences, is expressed in many ways. Poetry, writings of mystics, other art forms, are just some of the expressions that can seek to indicate an awareness that is at once immediate and transcendent. Boehme describes the realization of such dialectical insight as the lifting or raising of consciousness into the

106

supersensual level; Buddhism refers to it as enlightenment; and Christianity calls it sanctification.

These terms, and others with similar implications, refer to a transformation of the data perceived and the functional possibilities of the perceptive organism. It is therefore a change of both the sensory inflow and the behavioural outflow, and the dual aspects of the two-way process basic to egoic function are simultaneously radically modified.

Thus an egoic zone becomes an instrument hammered into shape on the anvil of time. Instead of being a non-comprehended lump of insensate metal, it becomes a javelin forged by conflict and made a tool of the Logos, using here the Christian term for the pre-creative word of God.

Such a transformation is the result of intense concentration of the forces of being to the point where ordinary psychological and physiological processes are transcended. Instances of such a conversion have at times been reported by people experiencing extremes of fear when completely new sensations and insights have arisen. A change of this nature is a pointer to the process of fulfilment here considered. Egoic transformation both affirms and negates the ego. It affirms it Absolutely, but negates the empirical reliance on formal aspects of its structure. Thus it opens the way to completely new levels of operation and the egoic focus may then aptly be described as 'paradoxical'.

Egoic fulfilment is therefore neither an end point with escape into a nebulous bliss, nor the attainment of empirically defined objectives. Instead it is the advent of greater functional possibilities, or in short, a new beginning.

Chapter 7: Towards Attainment

The ongoing nature of evolution implies that the ideas expressed in this study, like any other formal presentation, are subject to review and revision. But they are shared in the hope that they will contribute to ongoing research of the subject. The same principle applies to the insights presented in this final chapter as we review steps that some of us have found helpful in the ongoing search for Self understanding and fulfilment.

The five-fold analysis of the power operant within us that has been applied throughout this study has regularly helped many of us pursue this quest. And it can again be a useful guide as we now reflect on and summarise the aids to our ongoing search.

As always, the will is our starting point. We may use various terms to describe it; initiative, creative intention, volition are a few widely employed. Immediately we are encountering the difficulty of describing in words an awareness of the moment. To aid consideration of this aspect of consciousness we have previously likened it to interest unfettered by prior conditioning. Whatever terms we apply, we are seeking to describe an imperative that is itself unseen, yet is implied by the results of its action within us. Which means that careful studies of our psychological and physical experiences can reveal the operation within us of the invisible initiative we describe as will.

Our next step is therefore to focus again on the relatively gross expressions of power in the physical realm. Since this is the medium in which other aspects of awareness are revealed, it is obviously important to take due care of it as well as reflect on the insights it can yield. Hence we may remind ourselves again of the importance of appropriate diet, exercise and sleep regimes. Whether we are pursuing insight through regular daily tasks, or specific exercises developed over centuries of human experience to assist personal energy flow and understanding, the physical form is our vehicle of experience. Due attention to its practical needs is therefore a starting point in our pursuit of understanding and fulfilment.

Our reflection on the power involved in physicality depends on, and at the same time investigates, sentience. It is the key to the assessment we make. Whether it is a simple like/dislike assessment and reaction, or more subtle modes of evaluation and expression, the innate sentience of our being is our guide.

We may learn to watch reactions evoked and through them trace conditioning that otherwise could incur an unchecked bias on our experience. Reflections of this nature can have dual benefits. Whilst it releases from restrictive bias, the process involved can also enhance other aspects of personal insight.

For example, a woman who experienced recurrent depression found that it was provoked by particular family interactions. Investigating this reaction with the help of a psychotherapist, she recalled that the recent family events had reactivated memories of her Father's death many years previously and aroused emotions provoked but not adequately expressed at that time. In the therapeutic setting she was able to recall the events and release associated emotions in a way that helped her, not only ease the previously in-held tension, but discern more clearly how the reactions she felt then had subsequently influenced her assessments of other family members and situations. This new insight both eased her reactions and helped her see the other family members with less bias. But the insight also went deeper. As she recalled the death scene, in a tone of marked surprise, she suddenly verbalised an awareness that her Father was electing to die at that moment. That brief insight into the operation of individuated will proved to be a major turning point in her therapy. Through tracing her innate awareness, she had not only released significant inner tension, but had gained new insight that aided her personally and her interactions with her family.

In order to express the sensory impressions perceived we use linear thoughts and verbalisation. The words are vehicles for understanding as they formulate the awareness perceived and help clarify the insight they are used to represent. This means that concepts can have a two-way effect. Whilst they outwardly express an inner sensitivity, their feedback supports continuing reflection on yet finer levels of awareness. Throughout human history reflection on concepts associated with human development has assisted a growth of consciousness. Ideology may serve as a tool which, when actively applied, can be used to enhance the insight into dynamic processes too quick for complete definition.

Even ideas that we deem unacceptable can contribute to ongoing development. By closely observing concepts we find alien to us, we may find greater insight into conditioning that could otherwise maintain an unquestioned effect. Latent pressures such as emotional attraction or repulsion, and ideas that seem to direct a personal sense of power, prestige or wealth, are just some of the factors that have been found to influence a personal hold on certain concepts. Careful review of such incentives has often assisted a clearer decision on whether to retain or modify previously held ideas. And, if to a less biased view an idea is still regarded as erroneous, a thorough clarification of its apparent deficiencies can support newly developing insight.

But if these are possible effects of unacceptable concepts, what may be said of those that, at least for the time being, are assessed as valid? The active acceptance of an idea can help prepare a being for greater insight into the awareness it denotes. A concept operating in this manner is a type of prophecy, preparing the way for progressive realization of the aspect of power that it represents. This is the active and immediate application of ideology to which we have referred at greater length in previous chapters. It at once affords a plan, or self-definition within sentient power, and acts as a stimulus to enhance the awareness even of the non-definable aspects of the power continuum it seeks to represent. This process, as personal experience reminds us, will always be more efficient when ideas are clearly expressed. Hence the importance of precise terminology.

Whilst such an active use of formulation is progressively discerned, the awareness is also heightened that lapsing into inertic repetition could impair insight. So we need to become more alert to avoid falling back into such restrictive practice.

Such alertness is particularly needed when we use defined practices to aid our research. Throughout human history there have been reports of the ways in which careful use of practices such as precisely pursued ritual, mystery plays, prayer, meditation and diverse

110

forms of worship have assisted a personal growth of Self understanding and function. These practices, and other similar aids to personal research, are still widely available today. But like any activities we pursue, their role in enhancing Self awareness depends on the degree to which they are understood or governed by unquestioned inertia.

Any practice can be enlightening or restrictive. If its use is governed by unquestioned repetition, it necessarily limits new insight. But actively used it can greatly assist insight into dynamics that operate constantly.

This brings us again to the principle that understanding is momentary. Ongoing development requires a constant readiness to adapt to new insight. We have noted recurrently that adaptability is vital to continuing understanding and functional fulfilment. A person whose equilibrium depends heavily on a specific life style, restrictive relationships, or unquestioned ideas, is clearly more vulnerable and impoverished than one who can adjust quickly to change. Such quickening adaptation is a fundamental aspect of increasing Self understanding and egoic fulfilment.

We are now referring to the awareness we have previously considered as 'comprehensive'. The term implies a personal ability to apply concepts, evaluate emotions and function physically in relation to a constantly changing environment.

Comprehensive insight is a growing consciousness of the immediacy to which we have referred recurrently in this study. Such an instantaneous awareness of the dynamism operant in a situation is clearly very much faster and finer than any linear formulation can adequately describe. But here again, the ideas relating to its occurrence, despite their limitations, may serve a prophetic function in preparing a being for a greater realization of the awareness they indicate.

In the course of such reflection glimpses may begin to emerge of a highly alert awareness that sharply contrasts the linear, empirically biased experience usually known. It is described as 'comprehensive' because it affirms the immediate co-operation of the five-fold modalities of power we have been considering. It is a psychosynthesis, an integration of aspects of consciousness simultaneously discerned but not divided. As such awareness begins to dawn there is an increasing realization that any prior separation has been apparent rather than absolute.

Here the dialectic of consciousness is made clearer. Whilst there is an instantaneous awareness of the synthesis and non-duality of its modalities, simultaneously there is recognition of the particular aspects of consciousness that could be emphasised by relative stress. Thus the five-fold analysis and synthesis of consciousness are both affirmed in a new way.

Such insight is a realization that personal security and egoic fulfilment can only be found in the return to the innate, quick awareness of dynamic intentionality. That is, it affirms the momentary nature of understanding and the immediate re-position of the physical and mental aspects of being in and through which it is expressed.

This intensified awareness is therefore not a negative type of introspection that might be expected to deny the relevance of physicality. It is its precise opposite. It is a realization of the understanding clarified by Self opposition of power. That gross substantial impactions, sensory assessments, formulated names or concepts, the integration and initiation of all these and more, are likewise contributing to an increasing consciousness of consciousness. In this way it pays due heed to all its aspects, including the paradoxical ego, which is simultaneously affirmed and transcended. Such insight affirms that commitment is the key to fulfilment.

Therefore, in approaching a level of consciousness aptly described as 'transcendent' we learn that thorough, immediate application to the act of the moment is the way to greater fulfilment.

And the end is the beginning.

Index

www.ingramcontent.com/pod-product-compliance
Lightning Source LLC
Chambersburg PA
CBHW051026030426
42336CB00015B/2744